THE
TIE
THAT
BINDS

a marriage revolution of love

Debra White Smith

CONTENTS

*The definition of insanity is doing
the same thing over and over
again and expecting to get different results.*

ALBERT EINSTEIN

Are You Ready for a Revolution?

Daniel and I got married more than 28 years ago. I tell everyone I was 12 and Daniel was 16. Really, we weren't much older than that. I had been 19 for 12 days, and Daniel was 2 weeks away from 23. We were "babies." We had a lot of learning and growing to do, along with a lot of issues to work through.

But we hung in there. We grew up together. And by the grace of God, we became one...truly one.

Gradually we realized our marriage had grown into something spectacular—something most everybody longs for but few have—even in Christian circles. Daniel and I experience:

* high-level attraction
* loads of communication
* mutual respect
* tons of laughter
* great romance
* exhilarating sex
* best friends intimacy

How did we attain this remarkable relationship? Interestingly, we didn't get there through a door marked "Tradition." Instead we got there through a door marked "Revolution." Our journey began when I started seeking God with my whole heart for hours a week and sometimes hours a day. I stumbled into the practice of simply sitting, of being still, of listening for God's voice. There wasn't a lot of talking on my part. No, I didn't hear external voices or get loopy or psychotic. But in my soul and spirit I fell silent and made myself available for God to share His wisdom with me. Jeremiah 33:3 says, "Call to me and I will answer you, and will tell you great and hidden things that you have not known" (Jeremiah 33:3 NRSV). I can tell you from experience that God can and does exactly this.

When I brought my marriage before the Lord, He impressed upon me one of Christ's key exhortations: "In everything do to others as you would have them do to you" (Matthew 7:12). The Lord took me straight to the words of Jesus as an answer to the cry of my heart for more excitement, more romance, and much-needed healing in my marriage. So I dared to live out Matthew 7:12. I started romancing my husband with great gusto because I so wanted him to romance me. My book *Romancing Your Husband* is an outgrowth of this dynamic learning time in our lives. Thousands of women have reported healing and recovery in their marriages after putting the principle of romancing their mates to work. And then Daniel and I wrote *Romancing Your Wife*. Again, many couples found new life in their marriages. I highly recommend these books to add sparkle to your marriage. The profound impacts of these books and their contents and the amazing growth Daniel and I—and others—experienced didn't happen because I'm so smart. They happened because God is so smart.

Marriage Revolution is also a result of sitting before God, listening to Him, extensively studying His Word, and encountering other people who had marriages that reflected traits I wanted in mine. I don't hold a Ph.D. in psychology or biblical studies, although I am educated and well-read. I'm a woman, a writer, a Christian speaker, and a wife who wanted her marriage to be the best it could be. When Daniel's and my marriage grew into a thrilling, spectacular adventure, God led me to write this book.

One insight I discovered with God's help is that so many times we approach the Word of God with our dysfunctional issues in full swing. Instead of letting the Word of God impact our issues and bring us into balance spiritually, emotionally, and mentally, we allow our problems to impact the Word of God. We inadvertently mold the Word into a shape that confirms our issues or avoids them. From there we build marriage concepts and guidelines now based on faulty knowledge and understanding. Our issues may include cultural, gender, and racial prejudices; spiritual, emotional, and physical abuse; the need for control; the desire to manipulate; validation of a victim mentality; and one-upmanship. And that's just for starters. People can find and misuse Scripture to support these issues...and many, many more.

Often when the topic of marriage is approached, we start at the wrong place for what a Christian marriage should be like. We start with what we grew up with or saw portrayed around us (our culture), sometimes even going back to the "good old days" for inspiration. Then, when we read the Word of God, we emphasize the Scriptures that support our preset take on marriage and ignore or minimize Scriptures that contradict our views.

Depending on what poll you look at and what geographical location the poll reflects, Christian marriages are failing at a rate higher than, equal to, or slightly less than non-Christian marriages. This shouldn't be happening. Christian marriages should be stronger and more fulfilling because of our relationship with God and the Holy Spirit through Jesus. So why are our marriages falling apart? I believe a large part of the problem is what some churches are teaching on marriage.

The people who cling to traditional, culture-based concepts are well meaning, I'm sure. They love the Lord and truly believe they are teaching and modeling God's will. I don't believe people in the church are setting out to harm marriages. The traditionalists believe their principles are based on God's design. And yes, a few of these marriages appear to function well. Unfortunately, "God's design" often gets interpreted based on previously held beliefs or the cultural norms from yesterday or today. But marriage can be so much more than a fixation on who is in charge and living with the constraints of extraneous roles and rules. And when the church's silence or embarrassment on sexuality is added to the mix, Christian marriages are often at risk from the start.

Where are you in your marriage? Do you yearn for more closeness, more connectedness, more of a love affair? Are you willing to examine yourself honestly to see if you've inadvertently embraced prejudices and cultural preconceptions? Are you ready to confront personal views that may be influencing your understanding of Scripture? In the New Testament Jesus Christ cleared the temple because the people had gone astray in their practices. Are you willing to allow Him to "clear your temple" of any takes on marriage that might be hindering yours?

According to Webster's dictionary, "revolution" means "a sudden, radical, or complete change."[1] A revolution happens in our lives only when we're willing to set aside the current situation and fully commit to a new, exciting course. When most married Christians dare to be 100-percent honest, they often admit they don't have a phenomenal marriage and aren't "wowed" by their unions. If you can relate, why keep doing the same things over and over and expecting different results?

Dare to embrace change! Daniel and I have experienced our marriage revolution because we allowed God to breathe His fresh insights into our hearts and our home. We prayed, listened, and studied God's Word, setting aside as much of our preconceptions and cultural biases as we could. We took the chance and approached our marriage with open minds, open hearts, and mutual concern and love. We were gentle but honest with each other. And then we stepped out. We put into practice what we were learning.

Although we're certainly not perfect and we have our ups and downs, Daniel and I have a marriage that is beyond anything we ever imagined. It's over-the-top in love, exhilaration, satisfaction, cooperation, flexibility, and godliness. And our union continues to grow daily as we honor and serve the Lord and each other.

I encourage you to explore the path we've taken...and try it for yourselves. You won't regret it!

In Him,

Debra

Jesus is the Tie that Binds

*"Though one may be overpowered,
two can defend themselves.
A cord of three strands is
not quickly broken."*

ECCLESIASTES 4:12

Recently I booked an engagement for a marriage event. During the conversation I explained that I start with the teachings of Jesus Christ. I don't interpret any Scriptures in a way that contradicts or violates the teachings of Christ. The response from the booking person was the same one I've received many times: "Oh good. I'm so relieved. Thank you. This is so refreshing. It sounds wonderful!"

When God began to open my mind and heart to the concepts in this book, I honestly thought I was alone in my journey. When He impressed me to start sharing these revolutionary principles, I was terrified I would be "stoned" for daring to present a new model of marriage. But I obeyed God. The results have been eye-opening. I haven't been pilloried at all. More often than not, I've been applauded by men and women who express relief.

Surprisingly to me, some of the applause has come from couples who have gray in their hair and have been married many years. I've finally come to understand that many couples who stay together for several decades eventually grow into the Marriage Revolution model. They may not call it that. They may even still identify their marriage as "traditional hierarchical," despite the fact that neither the husband nor wife makes any major decisions without consulting the other and coming to a mutual agreement. But they've outgrown the "traditional" label without realizing it. What they're really experiencing is "revolution."

They've learned, as Daniel and I have, that a solid marriage involves a servant's heart and mentality from *both* spouses—a focus on the other person, selfless giving from both parties, and decision making by consensus. This attitude also impacts the romance of a marriage. In a high-romance marriage there is no thought of "I'm in charge" or "It's my way or no way," which in effect diminishes one spouse before God and in the home. To fully achieve the most exciting marriage, both spouses must be willing to fully embrace the teachings of Jesus Christ and apply them to their marriage. Ecclesiastes 4:12 says, "A cord of three strands is not quickly broken." In a Christian marriage, Jesus Christ is the third cord. He is the tie that binds. Show me a marriage that is exhilarating and exciting after 30 or 50 years, and I'll show you a couple who is living the revolution—of love that Christ taught— no matter what label they place on it.

Around the church there are several takes on marriage, and ministries often espouse different philosophies. What often happens is that well-meaning people who love the Lord unknowingly develop concepts based on a particular time or place in culture, and then go to the Word of God and emphasize key Scriptures that validate those teachings. When we analyze history and discover what cultural norms were at any given time, more often than not what the church taught on marriage has been in close alignment with the culture. For instance, when men had the legal right to beat their wives, the church supported that. When slavery was acceptable, Scripture was used to buttress that practice. What the church has taught on marriage through the years has changed as culture has changed. In this process, the teachings of Jesus Christ have often been explained away or twisted to conform to and support societal norms.

Today in western culture there is a push toward encouraging women and girls to believe they are better than men. This wrong attitude can only be supported with Scripture by isolating key verses and ignoring what contradicts them (see chapter 4). I've known and seen Christian women adopt female chauvinistic attitudes toward men in general and their husbands in particular. It's hard to genuinely romance your husband when you believe he is inferior. And most husbands whose wives don't respect them don't feel propelled to pour a lot of energy into the romance of their marriages. Many times these men will develop major hobbies that essentially become their mistresses. Or, even worse, they find living, breathing mistresses.

In the 1950s American society generally promoted the belief that men were "better than women"...or at least had more direct authority. The husband is the final decision maker on all matters, and the wife's role is to value his views and needs more than her own. This view is the "traditional hierarchical" marriage. It places the husband over the wife, in a way putting him one rung, or several rungs, higher than the wife in God's eyes as well as in the eyes of both spouses, despite the fact that Christ repeatedly told his disciples not to even think in terms of hierarchy. Both husband and wife are valued for their separate and distinct roles, but the husband's opinions and decisions are valued more. Key Scriptures are used to validate these concepts. The downside is that exhilarating godly sexuality isn't experienced. Wives tend to put very little energy into the sexuality of their marriages because they view their husbands as more father or authority figures than lovers.

The Equality Model of marriage is influenced by the cultural push from the last 40 or so years. We've heard a lot about equality between the sexes, and we're hearing more and more about equality in marriage. Quite a few churches promote this. There is much in Scripture that teaches God created men and women in His own image, and that we are all one in Jesus Christ. When spouses consider themselves true equals, they *do* have a better chance of experiencing high-romance marriages than the traditional hierarchical unions. Even though the Equality Model of marriage can be reasonably supported with the broadest use of Scripture, Jesus never once told anyone to *focus* on whether or not he or she was an equal. (See chapter 7, "Marriage Paradox.")

When Jesus is the tie that binds, marriage doesn't start with a particular culture base. Instead, it begins only with the teachings of Jesus. Although Jesus didn't say a lot about marriage specifically, He did cover general relationship concepts that should be applied to *every* relationship we have, especially marriage. If any marriage concepts we embrace contradict the letter or spirit of what Jesus taught, we need to reevaluate our beliefs. If we've used Scripture or had Scriptures cited as a basis for any beliefs not supported by Jesus' teachings, interpretation of those Scriptures needs to be looked at more carefully.

Balanced methods of biblical scholarship and interpretation happen when we begin and end with the teachings of Jesus Christ. Jesus' main teachings stress servanthood, a lack of selfishness, and treating others the way we want to be treated. Any time a spouse adopts an attitude that is self-elevating, self-seeking, or places the other spouse in a "lesser" position by devaluing the other's opinions or areas of expertise, he or she has limited or damaged the marriage and inhibited chances for an exhilarating union. High-level romance and a great sex life center on *choosing* to please and elevate your spouse. When both spouses take themselves off the throne of the home and marriage and place Jesus Christ there, miraculous things happen!

I recently shared the Tie that Binds principles with Christian psychologist David "the Relationship Doctor" Hawkins. He said, "Debra, you've hit the nail on the head. Most couples who come to me for counseling are in a battle for control and territory."

Embrace the Tie that Binds!

Allow God to perform a revolution in your marriage! Open the door to fantastic romance and an exciting bedroom life by wholeheartedly embracing the teachings of the greatest revolutionary who ever lived— Jesus Christ! Jesus marched into history and turned the tables on contemporary mores. He healed the blind, the maimed, the epileptic, and did so even on the Sabbath, a violation of the Jewish faith He was born into. He actively loved outcasts, forgave adulteresses, and hung out with the wrong crowd—tax collectors and prostitutes. He carried on significant conversations with women, which was taboo because women were tightly controlled and restricted by men and religion in those days. They were permitted conversations with only husbands, family, and other women.

As if these nontraditional actions weren't bad enough, Jesus also challenged the abusive religious leaders. He got in their faces, called them vipers and fools in public, overturned their tables of commerce, and captured the allegiance of their followers. Thousands of people followed Jesus, hungering for His words and touch.

And the Jewish religious leaders hated Him for it. They plotted against Him. They arranged His crucifixion. And even then Jesus had the audacity to say, "Father, forgive them, for they do not know what they are doing" (Luke 23:34). How did He have the strength to say that *and* mean it? Because He was divine. He was God in the flesh.

If we truly believe Jesus was and is divine, we must allow His teachings to be our guide in *every* element of our lives. "In Him we live and move and have our being" (Acts 17:28). If we are to live and move and have our being in Him, it follows that our marriages are to reflect the same ideals.

What would happen if we allowed our marriages to live and move and have their being in Jesus? What if we *started* with the teachings of Jesus Christ as the foundation for what we believe and teach about marriage? What if we dared to dismiss any and all cultural preconceptions that didn't line up with what He taught? What if we interpreted all Scripture through the life of Jesus? Dramatic changes would occur. Lives would be turned upside down. A revolution would start...just as it did when Jesus lived on earth.

Since Jesus is the Son of God, His words are the logical place to start. His teachings become our measuring stick for marriage. Revelation 1:8 states, " 'I am the Alpha and the Omega,' says the Lord God, 'who is, and who was, and who is to come, the Almighty.' " Hebrews 13:8 says, "Jesus Christ is the same yesterday and today and forever." Likewise, biblical truths about relationships, including marriages, will remain constant, unchanged by cultural whims and relationship fashions—no matter the political climate, geographic location, or era. When we choose a "cultural norm" for a marital base and proclaim that as God's design, we restrict our willingness to examine and embrace pure truth. Ultimately that hinders His moving in our marriages and "making everything new" (Revelation 21:5). God has been present from infinity in the form of the Father, Son, and Holy Spirit, and He will remain such into infinity. We need to allow *Him* to shape us and our marriages into *His* image, rather than shaping Him into the image of our culture.

If and when both spouses commit to living, breathing, and moving in the words and spirit of Jesus, the same thing that happened when He walked the earth can and does happen in marriages. A revolution of love sweeps into your union.

- God is free to be God.

- Jesus is free to be Lord.

- The Holy Spirit is free to flow through the marriage and home to heal and deliver and empower.

- Both spouses experience a taste of heaven.

Revelation 21:23 NKJV states, "The city had no need of the sun or of the moon to shine in it, for the glory of God illuminated it. The Lamb is its light." Jesus Christ said, "I am the light of the world. Whoever follows me will never walk in darkness, but will have the light of life" (John 8:12). When Jesus is fully allowed to be Lord in homes and marriages, His light from heaven explodes upon a marriage, transforming and renewing it. Admittedly, this is usually a *process* with couples, just like it was with my husband and me.

When Daniel and I got married, we had enough issues for four couples. Many have divorced over fewer problems than we had. And we didn't start seriously working on our issues for 16 years. Once we started, our revolution took nearly a decade. For others, it's a much faster experience.

Whether a marriage revolution happens in a one-day deliverance or a five-year process, the primary issue is our willingness to allow Christ to begin a new work in us. "He who began a good work in you will carry it on to completion until the day of Christ Jesus" (Philippians 1:6). This passage applies to us as individuals and to spouses who are willing to let Him complete what He has started.

Are you willing?

If so, we'll start with the heart of what Jesus Christ taught. I encourage you to read everything Jesus said with an openness to receive new understanding. Because of book limitations, I'll be focusing on specific passages that reflect the thrust of His overall messages. Remember, Jesus taught in broad generalities. He didn't say a lot specifically about marriage or parenting or even friendship. Instead, He made a good number of powerful statements that we are to embrace and apply to every relationship we have.

Consulting the Revolutionary

And he said: "I tell you the truth, unless you change and become like little children, you will never enter the kingdom of heaven. Therefore, whoever humbles himself like this child is the greatest in the kingdom of heaven."

MATTHEW 18:3-4

* "This is My commandment, that you love one another, just as I have loved you" (John 15:12 NASB). Although Jesus is speaking to His disciples here, this commandment applies to all Christians, including husbands and wives. Because Paul exhorts husbands in Ephesians 5:25 to "love your wives, just as Christ loved the church," many say that sacrificial love is solely the husband's role. This is similar to saying salvation is a role. It also causes many Christian women to fold their arms and wait for their husbands to manifest this level of love. I've heard more than one woman say, "I'm not going to put any energy into my marriage until my husband shows me this level of love." This mind-set is dangerous and

one-sided, which is what often happens when Scripture is approached in a one-dimensional way to prove or justify a preconceived notion or desire.

Yes, husbands *should* sacrificially love their wives. Most wives long for this level of love with every fiber of their beings. However, husbands long for that same level of love as well.[1] Jesus Christ commanded *all* believers to love unconditionally and sacrificially. The apostle Paul seconds this when he states, "Older women likewise are to be reverent in their behavior...that they may encourage the young women to love their husbands" (Titus 2:3-4 NASB). Scripture also says,

> Dear friends, let us love one another, for love comes from God. Everyone who loves has been born of God and knows God. Whoever does not love does not know God, because God is love. This is how God showed his love among us: He sent his one and only Son into the world that we might live through him. This is love: not that we loved God, but that he loved us and sent his Son as an atoning sacrifice for our sins. Dear friends, since God so loved us, we also ought to love one another. No one has ever seen God; but if we love one another, God lives in us and his love is made complete in us (1 John 4:7-12).

Commanding one spouse to love on a deeper level than the other is equivalent to saying one spouse should be more Christlike than the other. When *both* mates allow the miraculous love of Christ to flood their hearts, the result is a spilling out of that love upon the spouse and into the home. And that "love covers all sins" and works as a healing balm for past hurts (Proverbs 10:12 NKJV).

* "So [Jesus] got up from the meal, took off his outer clothing, and wrapped a towel around his waist. After that, he poured water into a basin and began to wash his disciples' feet, drying them with the towel that was wrapped around him" (John 13:4-5). In context this passage references how Jesus washed the disciples' feet. After doing this, He told them this was the attitude they should have toward one another. Christ never told anyone to *strive* for or *obsess* about being equal. Instead, He commanded His followers to put themselves last and embrace a servant's heart. When *both* spouses focus on washing each other's feet and serving each other, the breathtaking Spirit of Christ is freed within the union. A pure and holy equality *does* emerge, but it is equality based on mutual servanthood rather than "an equal share in everything."

* "So in everything, do to others what you would have them do to you" (Matthew 7:12). This Scripture is closely linked to the concept of reaping what we sow. Throughout the New Testament, references are made to reaping and sowing. For instance, 2 Corinthians 9:6 states, "Whoever sows sparingly will also reap sparingly, and whoever sows generously will also reap generously." The way you treat people will be the way you are treated. The things you do to others will be done to you.

Notice that Christ said "in everything." Everything includes the marriage principles we embrace and the attitudes we have toward the opposite sex. Husbands should not interpret Scripture to create marriage concepts or roles for their wives they don't want applied to themselves. Wives should not adopt attitudes toward their husbands they don't want directed at them. Chauvinism, whether male or female, is destructive and sinful.

* "To the Jews who had believed him, Jesus said, 'If you hold to my teachings, you are really my disciples. Then you will know the truth, and the truth will set you free' " (John 8:31-32). I do a significant amount of Bible study and scriptural analysis. One of my recent projects includes cataloging everything Jesus said and did to unveil what a multifaceted person He was and the variety of ways He handled different situations. If we truly desire to be Christlike, we must study what He *said* and what He *did*. Sometimes Jesus was meek and mild. Sometimes He was blunt and wild (calling the Pharisees snakes and overturning temple tables and chasing money changers with a whip. What a holy chaos He created!).

Whatever the occasion, even when Jesus was washing the disciples' feet, He always spoke truth. One of the things Jesus repeated often was "I tell you the truth." In the King James Version this is stated "verily, verily." Jesus is "the way and the truth and the life" (John 14:6). When we accept Him and His truth we are set free from our sin and given the freedom to embrace an abundant life of truth—total truth (John 10:10). Just as the source of all truth sets us free, so *stating* and *living* the truth helps set us free (John 8:32).

I'm discovering that marriages—even Christian marriages—based on gut-level honesty are rare. Many marriages are bound up because one or both spouses are terrified to speak the truth. Very calmly saying, "This is what you did, and this is how it affected me," is a powerful way to break through long-entrenched dysfunctional behavior and emotional issues. Are you afraid to be that honest? You shouldn't be blunt and hurtful, of course. But you can be sensibly honest. Too many times in marriages and interpersonal relationships people get defensive when honest discussion occurs. Promoting an atmosphere of gentle honesty and acceptance counters defensiveness and allows change to occur. According to "relationship doctor" David Hawkins, "A review of the Gospels quickly reveals that Christ was a leveler" in his communication style.[2] What is a "leveler"? Virginia Satir states that people who are levelers speak congruently, which involves…

- choosing to be yourself
- being aware of what you feel, think, and want
- being able to communicate that genuinely to others
- living without undue defensiveness, posturing, or game-playing
- preferring to make real contact with others[3]

Basing our marriages on the teachings of Christ not only involves unconditional love, a servant's heart, placing the spouse first, and treating the spouse as we want to be treated, but also having the fortitude to be a leveler. Amazing things can and do happen when truth is unleashed.

I urge you to find a red-letter edition of the Bible. These Bibles put all of Jesus' words in red. Carefully read everything He said. Allow His words to penetrate your soul and mind to the point that you have His eyes and His heart. Then take a look at your marriage and what you believe about marriage through His eyes. You might be amazed at what you will see and the changes you will want to make.

When both spouses commit to these concepts, miracles happen. The two people become one in every sense of the word. When one spouse commits, the marriage will improve. If you are the only spouse who works on this now, don't lose heart. Begin treating your mate the way you want to be treated. Pour the energy into your marriage you wish your mate would. Get gut-level honest with yourself and your mate. Your spouse's seeing Christ in you and the changes in you will be more influential than you know. You really do reap what you sow.

Prayer Points

One person can make a difference in relationships.

DAVID HAWKINS

* Pray that Christ will show you what He sees in your mate.

* As you read the words of Jesus, pray that God will open your heart and mind to everything that can apply to your marriage.

* Ask God to open your heart and mind to His voice in regard to your marriage.

* Beseech the Lord to prepare your heart for a revolution.

* Pray that God will give you the courage to embrace change in yourself and your home.

Love and Romance

Practice the heart of Christ. Give your mate a foot massage. Slather on massage lotion and pat his or her feet dry with a new hand towel. Keep the towel in a special place so you both see it daily as a reminder to keep a servant's heart.

"In a love-based marriage, both partners commit to love like Christ, serve like Christ, and see their mate as Christ sees them.

Living Sacrifices

*Therefore, I urge you, brothers, in view of God's mercy,
to offer your bodies as living sacrifices, holy and pleasing
to God—this is your spiritual act of worship.
Do not conform any longer to the pattern of this world,
but be transformed by the renewing of your mind.
Then you will be able to test and approve what
God's will is—his good, pleasing and perfect will.*

ROMANS 12:1-2

My husband, Daniel, and son, Brett, once took karate classes together. When they earned their yellow belts, Daniel said that it meant he's had a yellow stripe down his back. What that yellow belt *really* meant, though, was that if you tried to hurt them, they'd take off that cloth belt and whack you. Seriously, even though they were beginners, they still learned some good self-defense techniques.

Because of Daniel's interest in karate, he developed an interest in Mixed Martial Arts Fighting. He's watched boxing on television for years, and I've often watched it with him. Now we're watching this new fighting. It takes place in an octagonal arena. Unlike regular boxing, these guys use several types of martial arts skills as well as standard boxing. While they aren't allowed to scratch, bite, pull each other's hair, or kick in the groin, nearly everything else you can think of is legal. The fights get very tough. In one match some poor guy got a tooth knocked out.

At the end of a lot of these matches, spokespeople come on and say, "Remember, fighting is a sport. It's not a way to solve problems. When faced with a challenge to fight, it's best to walk away if at all possible."

Civil War Marriage

One of Daniel and Brett's martial arts teachers holds high-level belts in several forms. The teacher tells the story of the night he was in a grocery store parking lot and a robber approached him with a short knife and demanded his money. The teacher laughed at him, at which point the thief attacked. The teacher defended himself. While his fighting skills were good enough to seriously maim or kill the bad guy, he showed restraint and hurt him just enough to end the fight. I'm sure the robber will think twice before trying to hold up someone again.

The belief in the possibility of a short decisive war appears to be one of the most ancient and dangerous of human illusions.

ROBERT LYND (1879–1949)

How does this relate to marriage? In marriage, fighting is not a good habit to develop. An atmosphere of conflict seldom promotes intimacy.

One spouse often has greater fighting skills than the other. These skills may include in-your-face yelling, intimidation, and verbal prowess that can corner the other spouse. The results are the same. One spouse is left emotionally incapacitated while the other walks off. That's no way to build a healthy marriage.

Marriages can be like one big civil war. The husband and wife step into the ring like two boxers ready to duke it out for territory. Instead of throwing physical punches at each other, couples resort to verbal punches, weapons of manipulation, power plays, silent brooding, and glaring. The main theme is, "Which one of us is going to have the most territory in this home and marriage…and what can I do to make sure it's me?"

Back in the "good ol' days," most marriages centered on the husband having all or most of the territory. The misapplication of Scripture was the weapon of choice. Even though a lot of wives were silenced, deep inside many of them were frustrated and resentful. They resorted to their own methods of warfare, which often involved manipulation. Even though it's easy to criticize such wives, *both* partners were really at fault for demanding their own way.

In 1 Corinthians 13:5 Paul states, "[Love] is not self-seeking." When a husband and wife love each other with Christ's love, they are focused on elevating their spouse and doing everything they can to empower their spouse. So what about Genesis 3:16? "To the woman [God] said...'Your desire will be for your husband, and he will rule over you.'" First, understand that this message from God came *after* Adam and Eve sinned in the garden.

There are a couple of different takes on what Scripture means by Eve's "desiring" her husband. Some say she desired her husband as a lover and friend, but because of sin Adam wanted to rule her. However, many noted theologians state that the word "desire" also has roots in the desire to rule. So God could be saying that because of the sin that entered Adam and Eve's hearts and the world, Eve wanted to rule Adam...and Adam wanted to rule Eve. This interpretation makes the most sense because sin entered the hearts of both Adam and Eve, and sin typically manifests itself the same way in both genders—self-elevation and the demand for one's own way, whether blatantly or through manipulation.

The beautiful oneness that was celebrated in the garden of Eden was shattered by the desire to rule and control each other rather than the desire to work together to manage creation as God originally ordained:

> So God created man in his own image, in the image of God he created him; male and female he created them. God blessed them and said to them, "Be fruitful and increase in number; fill the earth and subdue it. Rule over the fish of the sea and the birds of the air and over every living creature that moves on the ground" (Genesis 1:27-28).

After the creation, God gave Adam and Eve a joint assignment: to rule creation together…as a team…as a unit…as one. This assignment was not given to Adam alone, but to Adam *and* Eve.

Whether a person is male or female, the fallout of sin is the desire to rule, control, and manipulate. This destroys marriages. The reason God told Eve her husband would rule over her was not because this was his "God-ordained role" but because sin had entered Adam's heart and that's what sin does. It demands its own way, therefore, sin is the opposite of selfless love. When Genesis 3:16 is used as the foundation for marriage roles, the marriage is being based on the *fallout of sin,* rather than the *freedom found in Christ's redemption.* According to Joseph Coleson,

> Both the Old and New Testaments make it abundantly clear that one of the characteristics of the Order of Redemption is a restoration of the equality between male and female. The question for the Church becomes then, Are we going to perpetuate an order of male/female relationships that has its roots directly in the Fall, that is a direct and immediate consequence of sin, or are we going to live in the Order of Redemption, that clearly and intentionally calls us to gender equality?[1]

Jesus' ministry was based on servanthood, not on ruling. Saying that the husband's role is to rule the wife or the wife's role is to rule the husband is equivalent to saying it's one brother's role to kill the other brother because Cain killed Abel. Murder happened because of sin. So does the desire to rule.

Well-meaning people have taught that "the husband is to rule the wife because this is God's curse upon Eve…and ultimately on all wives." When women view their husbands and their relationship with their husbands as a curse, that pretty much ends or at least maims continual joy and delight. There may be occasional happiness, but usually wives decline putting energy into the sexuality and romance of marriage. They see husbands as a negative and demanding dynamic. Instead of the marriage being a blazing love affair, the husband and wife suffer from emotional deprivation and are prime targets for extramarital affairs. What a tragedy! Especially when we consider that marriage with Christ on the throne can be an exhilarating experience.

Putting Christ in His Place

In Galatians 2:20 Paul states, "I have been crucified with Christ and I no longer live, but Christ lives in me. The life I live in the body, I live by faith in the Son of God, who loved me and gave himself for me." Most mainline denominations teach that all Christians should, like Paul, count ourselves crucified with Christ. This means we take ourselves off the throne in our hearts and place Jesus Christ there. We stop ruling, and Jesus becomes Lord of our lives. The song "I Surrender All" by Judson W. Van DeVenter is a testimony of this experience.

> All to Jesus, I surrender;
> All to Him I freely give;
> I will ever love and trust Him,
> In His presence daily live....
>
> All to Jesus, I surrender;
> Make me, Savior, wholly Thine;
> Let me feel the Holy Spirit,
> Truly know that Thou art mine.
>
> All to Jesus, I surrender;
> Lord, I give myself to Thee;
> Fill me with Thy love and power;
> Let Thy blessing fall on me.[2]

We have a choice of leaving ourselves on the throne in our hearts, of staying in charge, or fully placing Christ there. Although some Christians make this choice upon receiving salvation, most accept Christ as Savior, and He gradually reveals that giving Him supreme position in every area of their lives greatly benefits them. When you get saved, it's not a question of how much of Jesus you have. It's a question of how much of *you* Jesus has. We eventually have to ask ourselves if Jesus is the resident or president of our hearts.

As we grow in our faith in Christ, God shows us more areas of our lives (and hearts) that we've been hanging on to. Sometimes this is a process of fine-tuning our surrenders. Putting God first in our lives is a continual process…and sometimes a struggle. As I'm sure you know, humans can be prideful, selfish, and stubborn. When we finally completely give the area in question to Christ, we usually experience relief and great satisfaction.

But there are also those situations where we run from God, just as Jonah ran from God's call to preach in Ninevah (book of Jonah). If we don't give Jesus His rightful place as Lord of our lives, we become spiritually shipwrecked. Lives can be destroyed because of sinful choices. The same thing can happen to marriages when Christ is not given His central place.

Then Jesus said to his disciples, "If anyone would come after me, he must deny himself and take up his cross and follow me. For whoever wants to save his life will lose it, but whoever loses his life for me will find it."

MATTHEW 16:24-25

Christians who are indeed crucified with Christ *daily* surrender their wills to Him and testify to a victorious and blessed walk with the Lord because Jesus has free access to their hearts. Like the biblical King David, they daily pray, "Search me, O God, and know my heart; test me and know my anxious thoughts. See if there is any offensive [KJV: wicked] way in me, and lead me in the way everlasting" (Psalm 139:23-24). And the same experience applies to marriage with the exact same results. When both spouses place Jesus Christ first, a victorious, strong, and breathtaking marriage emerges. Both individuals experience the saving grace of Jesus, and when disagreements crop up battles can be avoided. The couple can choose to bow before the Lord together and seek Him until He shows them His will. God wants us to have harmony and unity in our homes!

When couples locked in battle come to me for advice, I ask, "Have you surrendered your will to Christ? Next give Him your home and your territory. Stop pushing for your way or final say. Allow Christ's presence to permeate your marriage and seek His will wholeheartedly until both know and agree upon how to proceed." When we surrender our wills to Christ, we are free to surrender ourselves to our mates in a healthy and functional manner. Amazing things happen at this point.

Will the Real God Please Stand?

When Christ was on earth, the religious leaders had put into place many rules to govern almost every activity. Jesus confronted the leaders, saying, "You have a fine way of setting aside the commands of God in order to observe your own traditions! For Moses said, 'Honor your father and your mother,' and, 'Anyone who curses his father or mother must be put to death.' But you say that if a man says to his father or mother: 'Whatever help you might otherwise have received from me is Corban'(that is, a gift devoted to God), then you no longer let him do anything for his father or mother. Thus you nullify the word of God by your tradition that you have handed down. And you do many things like that" (Mark 7:9-13).

Jesus was condemning the use of tradition to get out of supporting aging parents who had no other means of support. He was essentially saying we need to be cautious about traditions and evaluate their value and validity.

Human nature is interesting. Most generations are marked by the older crowd rejecting the current norms and looking back to the "glory days" of how things were when they were growing up. For instance, in the 1940s people looked to the early 1900s as the ideal era. In the 1980's, the 1940's became the best era. Many times Christians have used the Word of God to promote a return to the cultural norms of yesteryear. In today's world, when the topic of marriage comes up, the major stress often isn't on relinquishing all to Christ but on "restoring" marriage to what it used to be in "the good ol' days." Many times this refers to the idealized 1950s, "Leave It to Beaver" era.

While some traditions are harmless, others are not. Many times we adhere to tradition because that's "the way it's always been." Scriptures are often chosen that specifically support a tradition, and we ignore or fail to mention those that contradict it. There is nothing holy about validating traditions that aren't in agreement with the heart of Christ. When people do this, culture, not Christ, becomes the deciding factor on what is accepted and promoted. In *The Christian Family in Changing Times,* Robert Hicks states,

> I have come to understand we do serious harm when we place a con-
> cept of roles upon people and ask them to obey a culturally accepted
> "Christian" set of behaviors. It's far better to do the WWJD [What would
> Jesus Do?] thing and ask, How would Jesus love this person? That's my
> responsibility.[3]

When we put tradition over God's teachings, tradition becomes a god-like
influence, or in some cases, a god within itself. If we aren't careful, cultural tradition becomes our truth instead of God's Word, just as it did for
the Pharisees. Many parts of today's world are more in alignment with
Christ than in the good ol' days, such as the promotion of racial equality.
But there are some things still out of whack.

As quoted in the opening of this chapter, Paul states, "Do not conform any
longer to the pattern of this world, but be transformed by the renewing
of your mind. Then you will be able to test and approve what God's will
is—his good, pleasing, and perfect will" (Romans 12:2). For generations
some people have improperly used God's word and commands to insist on
conformity to man's laws rather than the teachings of Christ. The results
on marriage are dysfunction, unfulfilling relationships, and often divorce.

Many times I've heard well-meaning people say there will be no peace in
the home or marriage until the wife understands that God has ordained her
husband to rule and her role is to submit to his rulership. Fifty to 100 years
ago this was as much a part of American culture as slave ownership in the
early 1800s. The husband was viewed as *many* rungs higher than the wife.
(Wives couldn't inherit, own property, vote, etc.) Interestingly, these marriage concepts seem to be more in line with some Middle Eastern views
on marriage than they are with the teachings of Jesus Christ. According
to David and Vera Mace, "To the Eastern mind, therefore, the difference
between the man and the woman was a basic difference.... By her very
nature she was secondary, auxiliary. This is the very root of all the dis-
crimination between man and woman that has characterized the history of
the East, and in earlier times, of the West as well."[4] The truth is, peace *can*
be accomplished when one person does all the submitting to another. And
it's not always men who dominate. I've seen men who submit to the ruler-

ship of authoritarian wives, and yes, there's peace in those homes as well. But this comes at a great price. According to Jack and Judith Balswick,

> Assimilation in marriage, where the personhood of one spouse is given up, is not Christian. Christian marriage is more like accommodation, where two separate people maintain their distinct personhood but agree to come together in unity and oneness of commitment, meaning, and service...In Christian marriage each partner is subject to the other: each is to love and be loved, to forgive and be forgiven, to serve and be served, and to know and be known. A marriage in which one partner, the husband or wife, is asked to give up his or her personhood for the sake of the other denies God's expression in and through a unique member of the creation. The relationship is remarkably more fulfilling when both persons are expressed equally through their union. This allows others the opportunity to know two distinct persons as well as the couple who have become one flesh.[5]

Whether the wife or husband submits to the domination of the other, there will be a form of peace, but there will not be solid emotional or marital health. Years ago many slave owners used the Word of God to validate owning people. They used the same formula as many have used to support husbands ruling their wives: Start with the prevailing cultural attitude and find Scriptures that support it. They demanded that slaves "fulfill God's Word" and submit to the rulership of their masters because the apostle Paul admonished slaves to do this in Ephesians 6. I am reminded of a line in the movie *Amazing Grace*. One of the black characters essentially said, "A brand was put on us to remind us that we no longer belong to God, but to a man." The slave owners took the place of God in the slaves' lives—even if the slaves didn't agree. When slaves submitted to the rulership of their masters there was calm, but deep inside a revolt was fomenting.

In authoritarian marriages, peace comes at the cost of a thriving love affair. Couples with strong, very-much-alive relationships who have one spouse dominating or ruling, are very rare indeed. (Frankly, I've never met one.) Instead, one spouse focuses on having his or her way and the other likely enables this self-centeredness. Sometimes this is blatant, but often it comes in the subtle insistence that one spuse has a "final authority" position. Over time, the other spouse gradually cedes more of him- or herself to the other mate and loses confidence and spirit. When women are underlings, they usually shut down sexually. Likewise, many husbands would withdraw from their wives if the Word of God were used to diminish them.

When we truly embrace Christ as the tie that binds, both husband and wife step out of the civil war. They remove themselves and culture from the throne of their marriage and home and release their territory to Jesus Christ. They look to Him as the ultimate decision maker. They view themselves as one under Christ. They desire God's will and His healthy peace more than they want their own way or dysfunctional calm. When these couples come to an impasse, instead of arguing, manipulating, or one person taking control and making the final decision, they seek God together until a mutual answer is arrived at. Neither partner forces his or her will on the other. Both are more interested in preserving the relationship than protecting their territory. Granted, this sometimes takes time and opportunities may be perceived as "lost," but the priority is the marriage.

Brian Nystrom calls this the Partnership Model and conjectures that this is the kind of marriage Adam and Eve had before sin entered their hearts and destroyed the unity of their marriage:

> In this partnership, I would imagine that Adam and Eve made decisions together and consulted with each other on everything. They would have communicated well, and one would not have ordered the other around. They did not selfishly meet their own needs at the expense of the other. They encouraged each other, and they spent time together. I visualize a marriage bond that was so close and mutually caring that they were inseparable—like one flesh. In a bond like this, it doesn't matter who's "in charge" because each party is so focused on the other that the needs and wants of both are naturally respected. Each partner respects the unique individuality of the other person.[6]

Every topic in this book is linked to these core issues. We'll look at numerous subjects that hurt and destroy marriages, from gender prejudices to dysfunctional coping mechanisms that people validate with Scripture. But none of these issues can be dealt with totally until both spouses surrender their wills to God and count themselves crucified with Christ.

I'm not saying that once a couple resigns all to Christ every problem or issue will vanish or they will never have another argument. We are in a lifelong process of sanctification in which God continually refines us. No one has "arrived." However, a complete surrender to the Lord places our hearts and minds in position for Him to begin working and correcting any problems that are hindering the marriage. In other words, we have to get ourselves out of the way so God can concentrate on delivering us from baggage and bondage.

I am thankful for devout Christian counselors and doctors who commit themselves to helping people find peace. However, Christ is the divine healer. He uses humans as His arms and hands, but only *He* can deliver you. In *Healing for Damaged Emotions,* David Seamands writes, "The Holy Spirit is, indeed, the divine counselor, the divine psychiatrist, who gets ahold of our problem on the other end."[7] I am continually astounded at the things the Lord shows me during my prayer time that He validates through books and people *after* I've already thought through the concepts with His guidance. God will guide you and help you work through issues as you pray alone or consult with a counselor, but He can best work in a fully surrendered heart.

If one spouse fully surrenders to the Lord it will make a marked difference in the marriage. A fighting match can only happen when both contenders step in the ring and declare that they are going to win. Likewise, a marital civil war happens only when *both* the husband and wife state they are going to battle for control. If a spouse walks away from the territory, that essentially leaves one partner "air boxing." Eventually he or she will realize the fight is off. Many times changes occur at this point.

Surrendering your will to Christ doesn't mean either partner should remain silent in the face of abuse, live without boundaries, avoid speaking truth about dysfunctional issues, or enable the other spouse to be self-centered.

There is a delicate balance to be achieved. However, I *do* know that when even one spouse fully surrenders themselves to Christ there is usually such a marked change that it impacts the other spouse and testifies to the astounding power of God's love.

Prayer Points

- Meditate on this: "I have been crucified with Christ and I no longer live, but Christ lives in me" (Galatians 2:20). Ask the Lord to show you any areas of your heart or life that aren't crucified with Christ.

- Pray that God will show you any traditions you've adopted as truth that aren't in alignment with the teachings of Jesus.

- Ask the Lord to give you the courage to reject any traditions that don't support or that violate His teachings.

- Resign "your territory" to Christ.

- Pray that God's perfect will be done in your home.

Love and Romance

List 10 reasons you love your mate. Include physical, spiritual, and character traits. Use your creativity in sharing the list with your mate. Write them on the bathroom mirror with a dry erase marker, send an e-mail, or put them in his or her briefcase. If you're really craft-oriented you can embroider the reasons on a pillowcase or carve them on a wooden plaque.

"In a love-based marriage, all control is released to Christ,
and the Holy Spirit is free to inspire and guide."

When Jesus Meets Our Issues

*The difficulty of marriage is that we fall in love
with a personality, but must live with a character.*

PETER DEVRIES

Words Women Use

I've heard a lot of men bemoan the fact they don't understand women.
If you're one of those men, then the following vocabulary words from
women will enlighten you. If you're a woman, feel free to share this list
with your husband to enable him to better understand your "special language."

> *Fine:* This is used to end an argument when women feel they are right
> and you need to shut up. Never use "fine" to describe how a woman
> looks. This will cause you to have one of those terrible arguments.

> *Five minutes:* This is half an hour. It is equivalent to the five minutes
> that your football game is going to last before you take out the trash,
> so it's an even trade.

> *Go ahead!:* At some point in the near future, you are going to be in
> mighty big trouble.

> *Go ahead (normal eyebrows):* This means "I give up" or "Do what you
> want because I don't care." You will get a "go ahead with raised
> eyebrows" in just a few minutes, followed by "nothing" and "fine,"
> and she will talk to you in "five minutes" when she cools off.

Go ahead (with raised eyebrows): This is a dare that will result in a woman getting upset over "nothing" and will end with the word "fine."

Loud sigh: This nonverbal statement is often misunderstood by men. A "loud sigh" means she thinks you are an idiot at that moment and wonders why she is wasting her time standing here arguing with you over "nothing."

Nothing: This means "something," and you should be on your toes. "Nothing" is usually used to describe the feeling a woman has of wanting to turn you inside out, upside down, and backward. "Nothing" usually signifies an argument that will last "five minutes" and end with "fine."

Please do: This is not a statement; it is an offer. A woman is giving you the chance to come up with whatever excuse or reason you have for doing whatever it is you've done. You have a fair chance with the truth, so be careful and maybe you won't get a "that's okay."

Soft sigh: This nonverbal statement means she is content. Your best bet is to not move or breathe, and she will stay content.

Thanks: A woman is thanking you. Do not faint! Just say, "You're welcome."

Thanks a lot: This is much different from "Thanks." A woman will say, "thanks a lot" when she is really ticked off at you. It signifies that you have offended her in some callous way. It's often followed by the "loud sigh." Be careful not to ask what is wrong after the "loud sigh" because she will tell you "nothing."

That's okay: This is one of the most dangerous statements a woman can make to a man. "That's okay" means she wants to think long and hard before paying you back for whatever you've done. "That's okay" is often used with "fine" and in conjunction with a "raised eyebrows."[1]

Even though this is humorous, too often men and women come to their marriages with a secret language they expect others to understand. Sometimes this code is used as a manipulative tool that can leave the spouse always guessing and walking on eggshells.

Many times this secret language is bred by unresolved issues that drive dysfunctional behavior. The truth is, before you get married, you spend time getting to know the person. After you get married, you get acquainted with that person's issues.

My kids are teens, but I'm already telling them they need to go through a good season of Christian counseling with their fiancés before they get married. Even though Daniel and I are savvy on making sure we work through potential issues with them now, we don't have a guarantee the parents of their future spouses will have done the same. Therefore, it's better to examine yourself and your intended for any issues and work through them before the marriage than to wait until after the marriage and be thrown into turmoil.

When Issues Impact Marriage

Unfortunately, everyone in the Christian community is not educated on the broad spectrum of emotional issues, what causes them, and how they affect marriage. Sometimes well-meaning church people turn everything into a spiritual issue, when some are really emotional issues or woundings from which people need deliverance and healing. Sometimes good-intentioned people are "rebuking the devil," when they need to be offering counseling. In *Healing for Damaged Emotions*, David Seamands states, "Some Christians see anything that wiggles as the devil…I spend a lot of time in the counseling room, picking up the pieces of people who have been utterly disillusioned and devastated, because immature Christians tried to cast imaginary demons out of them."[2]

Seamands further comments, "We preachers have often given people the mistaken idea that the new birth and being 'filled with the Spirit' are going to automatically take care of these emotional hang-ups. But this just isn't true. A great crisis experience of Jesus Christ, as important and eternally valuable as this is, is not a shortcut to emotional health. It is not a quickie cure for personality problems."[3]

Most mainline Christians believe that God is a trinity: God the Father, God the Son, and God the Holy Spirit. This trinity is broadly accepted to be three-in-one. Scripture teaches that human beings were created in the image of God. This reality brings us worth as God's children, but it also points out that human beings are three-part beings made up of Mind/Body; Soul; Spirit/Emotions. No, I'm not saying we're little gods. The holy trinity *is* the holy trinity. We are *not* the holy trinity or even *a* holy trinity. However, we are created in the image of God and because of that we are three-part beings. To be fully successful as Christians and in our marriages, all three areas need to be healthy.

We need to take care of our bodies through healthy diet and exercise. We should take any vitamins or prescribed medications that are necessary for maintaining good health. We need to commune with God and allow Him to have ultimate control of our souls and our lives and maintain a close relationship with Him. To have fully functional marriages, we also need to learn to recognize and receive healing for wounds to our spirits and emotions.

Some marriages are in dire straits because one or both partners have problems in one or all three areas, and all three areas must be dealt with before the marriage can be stabilized. For instance, if a person has a chemical imbalance in the brain, has addictions driven by emotional problems, and has a spiritual problem due to a lack of a commitment to God, all three areas must be addressed. Just addressing the spiritual side of the problem isn't going to make the chemical imbalance go away—barring God's miraculous healing touch. And my experience in such cases has been that He often uses medical doctors and medication to bring about healing, wholeness, and balance. However, all the medication in the world for a chemical imbalance of the brain isn't going to fix a spiritual problem or heal damaged emotions.

The Spirit/Emotions are often where so many problems hinge that can destroy marriages. Even if someone is wholly committed to Christ, he or she can still suffer from emotional woundedness that causes a perpetual case of missing the mark. When this takes on the shape of verbal abuse, false accusations, sexual addictions, or even a cloak of negativity, these and other issues can mar any chance of a vibrant and exciting romantic marriage.

David Seamands writes,

> Through fifteen years...letters and testimonies have confirmed my belief that there is another realm of problems which requires a special kind of prayer and a deeper level healing by the Spirit. Somewhere between our sins, on the one hand, and our sicknesses, on the other, lies an area the Scripture calls "infirmities."
>
> We can explain this by an illustration from nature. If you visit the far West, you will see those beautiful giant sequoia and redwood trees. In most of the parks the naturalists can show you a cross section of a great tree they have cut, and point out that the rings of the tree reveal the developmental history, year by year...
>
> And that's the way it is with us. Just a few minutes beneath the protective bark, the concealing, protective mask, are the recorded rings of our lives.[4]

For instance, if a man or woman was emotionally wounded as a child from a verbally abusive parent, then he or she will feel inadequate, unloved, demoralized, insignificant, and many times be blanketed by a spirit of fear. This person may spend his or her whole marriage reacting from these emotions rather than from reality. This woundedness can lead to a pattern of verbal abuse against the spouse, insane jealousies driven by fear of abandonment, easily hurt feelings due to feelings of inadequacy, and never realizing his or her own worth in the marriage or in life.

Depending on the level of emotional damage, this can do everything from plaguing a marriage with periodic upheavals to causing spouses to live in war zones. Neither scenario contributes to a healthy marriage and can kill chances of vibrant relationships.

Another problem that occurs many times is the issue of addictions—specifically pornography. Porn addictions start from a variety of reasons, such as a spiritual issue where Satan gains territory in a person's soul, curiosity that leads to deeper sin, a genetic predisposition to addictions, or a married man or woman who is sexually deprived and weakened to the pull of pornography. (And yes, women can be addicted to porn just like men.) Sometimes pornography is photographic and sometimes it's sexually explicit books that stimulate. Understand that none of these causes or the next one are mutually exclusive.

A major cause of porn addiction is using sexually explicit material as a coping mechanism to cover or deal with emotional woundedness. I was just talking with a friend whose marriage was destroyed by her husband's addiction to pornography and sex. She told me that the root of his problem was that he began using porn and sex as a means to cope with childhood issues linked to his father. He was already into porn for these reasons before they got married. Now that he is in recovery, he is discovering the root of the problem and is finally getting some help. But he lost his marriage before he could get past the denial and take action to get needed help.

Sometimes the people who get sucked into destructive coping mechanisms such as pornography, food addictions, or fear-based jealousies love the Lord with all their hearts. These people may be the most active church members on the planet. They may have asked God to purify their hearts and believe they are living in the fullness of all the Lord has for them. But in the midst of all the spirituality, these people struggle. No matter what they do, they feel they can't stop the sinful behavior.

These emotion-driven dysfunctions (sins) may end the chances of a thriving love affair within the bond of matrimony. Frankly, very few marriages aren't plagued by emotional woundedness. Our world is a tough one. And even if a person has the best parents on the planet who never wounded them, other kids at school can be beasts and leave a child scarred for life. Older children can emotionally and sexually molest younger children by invading their space and violating their boundaries. And many kids already have a pornography flirtation or addiction in full-swing by junior high because their classmates introduced them to it.

The answer to overcoming these issues lies in recognizing what dysfunctions are being manifested in the marriage, being honest and gutsy enough to admit them, and asking God to show you the root of the problem. From there, deal with the root. Ask for God's healing and wholeness. Commit to honesty and accountability. Seek regular, balanced counseling if necessary.

Regarding addictions, understand that some people testify to getting deliverance from an addiction to such things as substances or food or sex. But they're actually replacing the addiction with religion. They manifest all the compulsive tendencies that formerly bound them in their new, "acceptable" form of being the church workaholic and obsessing on religious issues. Often the church applauds them for their fierce "dedication to the Lord," which intensifies the addiction to religion. These people have not been delivered. They have *transferred* their addictive tendencies from one thing to another. They're still addicts. They still have a problem. They're just manifesting the addiction in a way the church tends to support. Most of the time God brings about true deliverance from addiction in a long-term process that involves professional counseling and a regular support group.

> *You will know the truth, and the truth will set you free.*
>
> JOHN 8:32

I believe it's God's perfect will for His children to have a blast in marriage... for husbands and wives to be best friends and lovers, enjoying a thrilling sex life that drives them closer to one another. Unfortunately I've discovered this wonderful relationship is far, far, far from the norm. Too many times this goes back to not understanding how vitally important it is to recognize how wounded emotions drive sinful behavior and dysfunctional coping mechanisms. When we are wounded, Satan steps in to capitalize on that woundedness. From there, he destroys.

When Issues Meet God's Word

When people with specific beliefs and actions encounter the Word of God, sometimes they create concepts that support those issues rather than allow the Word of God to impact their views. In the next chapter you'll see how many in the church used the Word of God to support prejudices of various kinds.

Any theology can be shaped to support issues. For instance, when people are emotionally insecure sometimes they focus on Scriptures that also imply an insecure relationship with God. Instead of a loving heavenly Father who wants to empower them to live victorious lives, God becomes an ogre eagerly awaiting Christians to blink wrong so He can ban them from heaven. This view creates a god of very little grace and mercy with no tolerance for a struggling Christian who is trying but may be still missing the mark on his or her road to recovery and deliverance. It's a perfect fit for emotionally insecure Christians who may have had a horrific parent who created the emotional insecurity. God becomes as terrifying and capricious as the parent.

On the other hand, when people have problems with self-control, they can create a theology that says it's okay to willfully and knowingly choose to sin all you want. Their motto? "Just go ahead and sin your brains out. You don't have to think about righteousness or living a holy life. God doesn't care!" In this theology, God is like a big, heavenly granddaddy who sets no boundaries, has no standards, and asks nothing from His children.

Neither of these extremes is healthy. Both views are carved out of the Word of God because the people who knowingly or unknowingly created them use the Word to support their preexisting issues. Then these folks flock to whichever churches support their warped views. They believe they've embraced "absolute truth" because it "feels so right" and "makes perfect sense." In reality, it "feels right" and "makes perfect sense" not because it's balanced theology that practically and logically consults the *whole* Word of God but because it supports their dysfunctions and ignores Scriptures that contradict them.

The truth is, God is a loving heavenly Father who will never leave us or forsake us (Hebrews 13:5). However, Micah 6:8 states that God does have requirements of us: "He has showed you, O man, what is good. And what does the LORD require of you? To act justly and to love mercy and to walk humbly with your God." According to Psalm 92:15 NKJV, "He is my rock, and there is no unrighteousness in Him." Since God doesn't walk in sin, walking humbly with God means we strive to fulfill Paul's command to "avoid every kind of evil" (1 Thessalonians 5:22). Willfully and knowingly embracing sin and saying God expects this is just as destructive as believing God's grace doesn't cover our human weaknesses when we do miss the mark. While there's no Christian on the planet who doesn't miss the mark and doesn't need God's forgiveness, that doesn't mean we should *purposefully* embrace sin or a sinful lifestyle.

Remember, a healthy view of our relationship with God isn't driven by issues, but by a careful, unbiased interpretation of Scripture.

When creating foundational teachings on marriage, a healthy balance can likewise be achieved by a sensible interpretation of Scripture that starts with Jesus Christ. If you're looking for a pure example of someone *without* issues, turn to Christ—not only what He said, but also what He did. Some Christians have an unbalanced take on what being Christlike means because they're not including what He *did*. If we're going to align our lives and marriages with Christ, we must embrace His complete life.

When we read about Jesus, our own issues can blind us to the powerful man He really was. We may be terrified of facing the stark truth head-on and coming clean with God and our spouse, so we "create" a Jesus who accommodates our fear and our "need" to remain silent about our problems or the things our spouses manifest. Jesus then becomes a predominantly meek and mild man who glossed over everyone's problems, patted them on the head, and said, "Oh well, sweetie, never mind that." According to this view of Christ, He never caused friction or had the audacity to state absolute truth.

In the 1800s William Blake wrote a now-famous poem called "The Lamb":

Little Lamb, who made thee?
Dost thou know who made thee?
Gave thee life, and bid thee feed
By the stream and o'er the mead;
Gave thee clothing of delight,
Softest clothing, wooly bright;
Gave thee such a tender voice,
Making all the vales rejoice?
Little Lamb, who made thee?
Dost thou know who made thee?

Little Lamb, I'll tell thee,
Little Lamb, I'll tell thee:
He is called by thy name,
For He calls Himself a Lamb.
He is meek, and He is mild;
He became a little child.
I a child, and thou a lamb,
We are called by His name.
Little Lamb, God bless thee!
Little Lamb, God bless thee![5]

Often, this is the take—and the only take—we have on Jesus. We view Him as a meek, mild lamb. However, Revelation also describes Him as the Lion of Judah (5:5). Many times in the New Testament, Jesus roared and created havoc like a giant-pawed, massive-maned lion who never backed down. He forever spoke absolute, gut-level truth and willingly confronted issues and abuse.

He was more than just a man.

He was God in the flesh.

He was a force!

Ecclesiastes says,

There is a time for everything, and a season for every activity under

heaven: a time to be born and a time to die, a time to plant and a time to
uproot, a time to kill and a time to heal, a time to tear down and a time
to build, a time to weep and a time to laugh, a time to mourn and a time
to dance, a time to scatter stones and a time to gather them, a time to
embrace and a time to refrain, a time to search and a time to give up, a
time to keep and a time to throw away, a time to tear and a time to mend,
a time to be silent and a time to speak (3:1-7).

Jesus Christ exemplified that there really is a time for everything. He did
many of the things that Ecclesiastes mentions. For instance, He challenged
the abusive and extraneous laws the Jewish leaders had imposed upon the
people, but He also healed the sick. He tore down traditions that fractured
God's love and law and built up those people who needed His touch. A few
times He was silent. Most of the time He leveled with people.

Sometimes He was as meek and mild as a lamb. He did lay down His life
like a lamb, but that was the ordained reason He came to earth. Nevertheless, He presented verbal challenges during His trial and never once
compromised truth. Every negative situation with Jesus was not a crucifixion. Neither should we view or enable every negative situation to become
a crucifixion in our marriages or in our personal lives.

Jesus Christ never enabled abuse. He made a habit of boldly and bravely
confronting abuse. When the money changers were taking advantage of
people in the temple, He stormed the place with a whip and overturned
their tables (John 2:12-16).

He showed love to sinners but absolutely never compromised the truth
of their sin. When He encountered the Samaritan woman at the well, He
treated her with respect and love even though she was of a race and gender
Jewish men traditionally despised. He was kind and gentle to her, but He
didn't avoid the fact that she had had five husbands and was currently
living with a man (John 4:1-26).

Jesus was honest about His emotions and how others affected Him. When
the disciples went to sleep instead of giving Him prayer support in the
garden of Gethsemane, He let His frustration be known (Matthew 26:36-

45). When He thought someone wasn't measuring up, He told them. He repeatedly called the disciples dull when they were unable to see with their spiritual eyes (Matthew 15:16). And when it came to the corrupt religious leaders, He *publicly* called them vipers, fools, hypocrites, and whitewashed tombs, one of the worst insults of the day (Matthew 12:34; 23:17; 22:18; 23:27-28).

Even though Jesus showed love and compassion to those in need, He also held people's feet to the fire and expected them to act in a mature fashion when they were corrected.

We don't have a license to arbitrarily overturn tables, be purposefully rude, stand up in a church service and call our pastors hypocrites in front of everyone, or unwisely create havoc. As already mentioned, Ecclesiastes says "there is a time for everything" (3:1). The key is finding God's wisdom in knowing when to be silent and when to overturn tables. Yes, Jesus did tell us to turn the other cheek (Matthew 5:39) and affirmed "blessed are the peacemakers" (5:9), but in observing what Jesus *did* we can't interpret these passages or any others to mean that we make peace to cover sin, turn the other cheek to habitually enable abuse, or pretend people are measuring up when they aren't.

Matthew 10 quotes Jesus, "Do not suppose that I have come to bring peace to the earth. I did not come to bring peace, but a sword" (verse 34). Either Jesus was saying He wasn't going to fulfill His own beatitude about being a peacemaker or there really is a time for everything…a time to make peace and a time to use a "holy sword." Hebrews 4:12-13 says, "For the word of God is living and active. Sharper than any double-edged sword, it penetrates even to dividing soul and spirit, joints and marrow; it judges the thoughts and attitudes of the heart. Nothing in all creation is hidden from God's sight. Everything is uncovered and laid bare before the eyes of him to whom we must give account." God is the one to whom we must give an account. He is the source of absolute truth. When couples are in bondage to long-term dysfunction, sometimes stating truth is far from a peaceful experience. But truth works like a sword, cutting away issues and giving marriages the chance to be restored and renewed.

The Old Testament is full of situations where God told people to confront sin or stand up to abuse just like Jesus Christ did later, as recorded
in the New Testament. For instance, when Goliath verbally assaulted the
Children of Israel, God sent David to defeat him. It took a lot of courage
for David to take his slingshot and stones and attack that giant. But with
God's anointing, he took Goliath down. Likewise, the "Goliaths" in our
marriages can be taken down when one or both spouses have the guts to
speak truth and overturn tables.

On Communication

Every situation in a marriage does not require a "Goliath" slaying. Sometimes Jesus simply listened to people. Other times He quietly told them of
their sin, and they listened to Him. If your spouse is tangled in long-term
addictions or defeating dysfunctions, then by all means talk to him or her
about it. But sometimes what is needed boils down to simply listening to
each other while truth is stated.

Communication is one of the key ingredients to a vibrant marriage. Creating a nondefensive atmosphere where positive communication occurs is
paramount to a healthy marriage. Yes, it can be uncomfortable when one
spouse honestly shares the pain the other has caused. The more mature a
person is, the more willing he or she will be to hear constructive information about the relationship. A pivotal sign of maturity is the strength and
willingness to be secure and admit when we've failed. The bottom line is
that we've all failed each other. No one is perfect. We all need continual
adjustment and growth. That's part of the process of being carved into the
image of Christ.

In our attempts to communicate my husband and I have sometimes
flopped around and failed miserably. Some miscommunications led to
verbal wars during our early marriage. Others have led to disappointment.
For years I asked my husband what he thought about a meal or how I fixed
my hair or other matters I wanted to hear his praise on. He'd say, "It's
okay." Well, to me "okay" meant below average. To him "okay" meant
"excellent." After more than a decade of marriage I finally asked, "What

does 'okay' mean to you?" He said, "Great! Excellent!" In that second years of frustration unraveled! And now I'm okay with his okay.

Christian Enablers

My daughter and I recently used a plastic bucket to wash our van. When we got through, I laid the pail on its side on top of the garbage can so the moisture inside could dry and any moisture outside would drip onto the garbage and not leave a puddle on the shelf.

Well, I didn't get around to putting the pail back, and eventually, people added garbage around it. The trash soon covered the pail, and it eventually became a significant support for the garbage. The garbage on top was depending on that pail to hold it up. When I removed it from the top of the trash pile, the garbage fell to the floor. I set the pail on its bottom. As long as the pail was on its side supporting the trash, it was of no use for what it was made for. But once the pail was sitting upright and no longer supporting the trash, the container could be fully used once more.

That pail is a lot like some spouses. They are holding up the trash for their mates. Sometimes it's the husband holding up his wife's "trash"; sometimes it's the wife holding up her husband's "trash." Both spouses become dependent upon that trash, and both are unable to function in the marriage to the full level God intended.

Every sin is the result of a collaboration.

STEPHEN CRANE

Often addictions, emotional or verbal abuse, sinful behavioral patterns, and even physical abuse torment marriages. These issues are the "trash." Many times one spouse is trapped in the addictive or sinful behavior, and the other spouse enables the addiction or sin by making excuses for the spouse, ignoring the problem, or refusing to confront the person. This is called codependency.

In *When Pleasing Others Is Hurting You*, relationship doctor David Hawkins mentions "external referenting" as the leading symptom of codependency. "External referenting" means defining yourself by the way other people value you. It means being completely preoccupied with what others think. If we don't have firm personal convictions about our own significance and worth, we will look to others to assure us that we are important to them.[6] When we look to others for our worth, we will jump through any hoop they hold up to please them—even if it hurts us.

According to Robert Subby, codependent families manifest the following characteristics:

* Don't feel or talk about feelings.
* Don't think.
* Don't identify, talk about, or solve problems.
* Don't be who you are—be good, right, strong, and perfect.
* Don't be selfish—take care of others and neglect yourself.
* Don't have fun—don't be silly or enjoy life.
* Don't trust other people or yourself.
* Don't be vulnerable.
* Don't be direct.
* Don't get close to people.
* Don't grow, change, or do anything to rock this family's boat.[7]

When we tangle an unbalanced view of Scripture with being an enabler, we create a codependent Jesus who never rocked anybody's boat. Then we convince ourselves that if we are going to be Christlike we shouldn't ever rock anybody's boat either—especially if we desperately need their approval. Thus we remain silent in the face of dysfunction. In marriage this often means that one spouse manifests the obvious issues or addictions and the other spouse quotes Scripture to validate ignoring those issues or addictions. Both spouses end up depending on the behavior or addiction. But the enabler has the Word of God mixed in the equation in a way that blinds him or her to the problem and cripples the marriage.

One of the reasons why the traditional hierarchical marriage can be unhealthy is because in some cases wives become codependent and enable sin or bad behavior in their husbands because the women believe they are fulfilling their "God-ordained role" to submit to everything their husbands do and every decision they make, no matter how destructive or emotionally unhealthy. For instance, I've heard women say that since Paul tells wives to submit to their husbands in Ephesians 5, they should never speak up—even if the husband destroys the family's credit, is mean to the children, or has addictions. The wives believe they're supposed to "submit," letting their husbands continue their behavior until the negative consequences cause them to change. Some people even say that if husbands tell their wives to do something sinful, God won't hold the women accountable because they were submitting to their husbands' authority. Back in the "good ol' days" these views were exceedingly prominent. Now, with more balanced teaching, even among those who cling to the hierarchical view of marriage, fewer wives are codependent or *as* codependent as they once were.

Perhaps the reason why some Christian women still support the hierarchical view on marriage is because it best accommodates their existing emotional issues and gives them "scriptural backing" to avoid speaking truth. For some, it's easier to go with the flow and submit—even tolerating sin—than it is to have a voice and be responsible before God for not speaking up when they should. And there are husbands who remain silent when they should confront issues as well. Whether it's the husband or wife who is silent in the face of addictions, sinful behavior, or emotional problems, both are enablers and both are responsible before God.

Pure truth does not support sin or dysfunctional issues. Truth is balanced and stands on its own because it is based on what the Son of God said *and* did.

When Honesty Encounters Issues

Jesus Christ was gut-level honest. He said, "You will know the truth, and the truth will set you free" (John 8:32). He was referencing Himself here, since He is "the way and the truth and the life" (John 14:6). However, it's also correct that stating truth helps set us free.

When one spouse is holding up the "garbage" for the other spouse, stating truth constructively begins the process of climbing down from the garbage pile and sitting upright before the Lord, ready to be filled with His presence. Getting this honest in marriage can be the equivalent of turning over the money changers' tables. Sometimes truth is messy! Remember when I removed the pail from beneath the garbage? Junk fell everywhere.

The whole ordeal also drew a crowd. Three of my herd of cats came to check out the noise and see what was going on. Likewise, when the enabler spouse stops holding up the garbage, a crowd may form. Some will tell the enabler he or she is out of God's will by standing up to the dysfunction and drawing boundaries. Others will applaud the spouse for making the change. Some just won't understand and will think the former enablers have gone crazy. Many of the latter group can be in the close family network. They too might be holding up somebody's trash. Fully entrenched enablers seldom applaud anyone breaking free of codependency because they think holding up somebody's trash is the way relationships should be or the way God expects them to be.

> *Yet a time is coming and has now come when the true worshipers will worship the Father in spirit and truth, for they are the kind of worshipers the Father seeks. God is spirit, and his worshipers must worship in spirit and in truth.*
>
> JOHN 4:23-24

Just as a broken bone that is healing crooked must be rebroken to be properly set, sometimes sinful or dysfunctional patterns in marriages must be broken for total, healthy healing to be accomplished. This takes courage and honesty. It requires breaking through a wall of fear. Does this sound too hard? Don't lose heart. You have a helper! Jesus Christ is available for all who ask.

I encourage you to step forward, embrace the power available through Christ Jesus, and begin the transformation of your marriage. If this means stating truth to your mate, then do it. Continual silence will only more deeply entrench the problems. If you need to seek professional counseling, then go—even if your mate won't.

Jesus never enabled sin. Neither should you. No matter how much you love your spouse, whether you're the husband or the wife, remaining silent when there's any kind of a problem that needs to be dealt with enables sin. Enabling sin makes us guilty of sin ourselves.

Note: If this chapter touches issues you face, I highly recommend Dr. David Hawkins' books *When Pleasing Others Is Hurting You* and *Dealing with the CrazyMakers in Your Life* (Harvest House Publishers). I also recommend David A. Seamands' books *Healing for Damaged Emotions, Putting Away Childish Things, Healing of Memories,* and *Freedom from the Performance Trap* (SP Publications). Seamands' books are available in a compilation volume titled *Healing Your Heart of Painful Emotions* (Inspirational Press).

> *Sometimes silence is not golden—just yellow.*
>
> ANONYMOUS

Prayer Points

- As you read the four Gospels, pray that God will open your eyes to the real Jesus.
- Ask the Lord to show you if you are an enabler.
- Ask God to show you if you are expecting your spouse to enable your dysfunction.
- Be honest with God and your spouse. Confess the garbage in your marriage—garbage you're holding up or garbage you're expecting your spouse to hold up.
- Pray for the courage to confront the fear that is keeping you silent.
- Ask the Lord to give you the courage to accept truth from Him and your mate.

Love and Romance

A while ago I was listening to a radio interview. The man being interviewed said that when you're struggling to stay close to your spouse and keep your family together, sometimes the answer isn't always less work. Sometimes the answer is incorporating your spouse and family into your work. If you and your spouse are struggling to find time to spend together because of legitimate activities you can't get around, compare calendars and see if you can merge your activities and obligations and do them together.

> "In a love-based marriage, both spouses are free
> to be honest, and issues that bind the heart in
> fear are dealt with and extinguished."

Ruling and Drooling

*Marriage is that relationship between man
and woman in which the independence is equal,
the dependence mutual, and the obligation reciprocal.*

LOUIS K. ANSPACHER

A few years ago my daughter came home from school saying, "Girls rule. Boys drool." I'd heard this saying among girls before and was amazed at how early it filtered to my daughter. She was only in second grade...and attended a Christian school. I became immediately aware of how gender prejudices impact the minds of children. And if those prejudices are allowed to take root, they can warp their minds for life. So I had three options: 1) I could remain silent and allow the prejudice to grow deep roots on its own, 2) I could throw some fertilizer on the prejudice by saying something like, "You'd better believe it!" 3) I could uproot the cancerous seedling that could affect my daughter's attitude for life and possibly hinder her marriage.

I took Brooke aside and said, "Nobody rules or drools around here. Boys are as good as girls and vice versa. We don't look down on the boys (my son and husband), and they don't look down on us."

My husband and I both teach this lack of prejudice to our children—whether in reference to race, economic status, or gender. We treat everyone with respect and purposefully choose friends from all races and walks of life. We live our beliefs at home and in our community.

Have any prejudices sneaked into your life? Often the roots of gender prejudice involve pain from actions of the opposite sex, possibly abuse or neglect. Many times it can be linked to the parent of the opposite gender or a bad experience in marriage. For instance, some women hate men because of being molested and neglected by their fathers or abused and tormented by their husbands. Likewise, some men detest women because of mothers who were verbally and physically abusive or abandoned them or wives who have been controlling and overbearing. Many times a dislike of the opposite sex is steeped in suppressed pain, scars, and tragedy. In such cases, there's a toxic wound in that person's soul that feeds the hatred. I encourage the injured one to seek a wise counselor as well as healing from the Lord. Otherwise the marriage will be shipwrecked before it leaves harbor.

Another cause of gender prejudices is linked to teaching from childhood. Proverbs 22:6 says, "Train a child in the way he should go, and when he is old he will not turn from it." That Scripture is packed with truth! Once people are trained in the way they go, they get in a comfortable pattern, and it takes a conscious effort or miracle from God to change them. For years African Americans and Caucasians were taught from childhood to distrust and despise the other race. This became so engrained that it's taken years to begin the healing and stop this learned behavior.

Tragically, sometimes prejudices are supported by wrapping them in Scriptures, which can chain the sin to the hearts and minds of those who have embraced the error as God's truth. One of Satan's primary forms of deception is convincing people their sinful attitudes or choices are fine, often misusing God's Word as validation. He did this when he twisted God's words and used them to trap Eve in the garden of Eden.

In the previous chapter, I talked about how silence perpetuates dysfunction and how gut-level honesty works like a sword to cut through and end it. Now I'm going to level with you. I've got to state a truth that might make you uncomfortable. But change occurs when we hear the truth.

Many healthy church groups agree that racial and economic prejudices are sin, but too many times we don't recognize that gender prejudices are just as sin-based. And just as slave owners used the Word of God to support their owning, torturing, and beating African Americans, so some churches use the Word of God to support restricting or subtly demeaning women. Sometimes this attitude is blatant. I've sat under more than one scorching sermon targeted at putting women "in their place" and encouraging men to exalt themselves. More often than not, though, the demeaning is kindly spoken and even gently encouraging so women will accept their "God-ordained role" of lesser importance in their homes, marriages, and even in the eyes of God.

In his book *Ordinary People, ExtraOrdinary Marriages,* Brian Nystrom states,

> I have seen many men who regard themselves as better, smarter, and superior to their wives. I have seen husbands constantly invalidate their wives, catalyzing entropy [disorder]. I have seen many wives deeply hurt by the actions of their husbands. I have seen many wives accept abuse from their husbands because they thought their role was to "take it and be submissive." I don't think God intended wives to be doormats. God created and intended women to be equal to men in all aspects of life, as we have seen in the Garden of Eden model of marriage.[1]

Many Christian men are kind and courteous. Not all men or churches use the Word of God to demean women. I am friends with and work with a number of Christian men who are *very* considerate and respectful. However, I have encountered enough Christian men who devalue women that I know gender prejudice is a problem.

I've also encountered a sea of Christian women in various religious denominations who are extremely tired of the Word of God being used as a subtle or blatant weapon against them. Just this week a friend called who was exasperated at a radio minister who slammed women and blamed them for much of the dysfunction in churches. Ironically, she had no idea I was writing on this subject. I calmly told her, "This has been going on for generations. You're just now waking up to it. Now that you're recognizing it, you're going to notice it more and more."

Where there are deeply engrained racial prejudices there will usually be deeply engrained gender prejudices. Holding prejudices is like nursing a cancer of the soul. When a prejudice thrives against one group of people, it will fill the soul and continue against other groups, often in different areas. Sometimes one of the other groups is the opposite sex.

Unfortunately, gender prejudices are still proclaimed as "biblical truth" by many. And women are too scared, too scarred, or too confused by the use of Scripture against them to speak up. Some confess they have stopped attending church because of the spiritual abuse against females. They've even stopped reading Christian literature because so much is twisted against women. Sadly, I've also heard reports of non-Christian women who went to church seeking the Lord and encountered gender prejudices that caused them to leave. These women have said, "If that is what Christianity is all about, I want no part of it." When one part of the body of Christ uses the Word of God to control, manipulate, blame, demean, or restrict another part, Christ is *not* glorified and people who need Him turn away.

These attitudes are just as wrong when directed at men. In our ministry travels, Daniel and I have encountered Christian women who were rude to him because he was male. He sensed the tension and couldn't miss the pointed glares. This discouraged him, especially when he goes with a servant's heart to sing and empower all people.

And I've heard more than one Christian man express disgust at the contemporary sitcoms and movies that make men look like buffoons. So while the prejudices against women are prominent around the church, there are also obvious prejudices against men. And when wives hold these prejudices against their husbands, it can be just as destructive to marriages as husbands who demean their wives. This demeaning often occurs via misuse of Scripture or simply devaluing their spouse's contibutions, opinions, and God-given gifts.

Speaking frankly, there *are* some passages of Scripture that suggest husbands rule and wives drool. (For a fresh look at these and other passages, see chapters 5 and 6.) And there are also passages that can be used to "prove" that women rule and men drool.

A Case in Point

Understand that every scriptural reference and word meaning in these paragraphs are valid and true but were never meant to be used to elevate women over men or demean men. I am doing so *only* to prove the point that Scripture can be misused to validate gender prejudices. I *do not* agree with or support the following mindset in our ministry or anywhere else.

I value, appreciate, and work with men. I adore and highly respect my husband and have a loving, earth-moving relationship with him. I honor my son and pray that he doesn't marry a radical "femi-nazi." I also have a great relationship with my father, a retired minister, who doesn't believe the Word of God should be used to validate prejudices. He taught me by words and example to honor and respect all men and women. Furthermore, he cheers me on in my writing and speaking on this subject.

Now, for the prejudicial commentary.

The Bible is clear about the value of women over men, and references to this truth can be found throughout Scripture.

> "But for Adam no suitable helper was found…Then the LORD God made a woman from the rib he had taken out of the man, and he brought her to the man" (2:20,22). When God stated there was not a helper suitable for Adam, the word used for "helper" is the same root as what's used in Psalm 33:20; 70:5; and 121:2 for God. From the beginning of time, God placed the woman as His personal representative in the man's life. Consequently, husbands should go to their wives to find God's will and what He wants to speak to them.

> Proverbs 4:6-9 supports this by personifying wisdom as female: "Do not forsake wisdom, and she will protect you; love her, and she will watch over you. Wisdom is supreme; therefore get wisdom. Though it cost all you have, get understanding. Esteem her, and she will exalt you;

embrace her, and she will honor you. She will set a garland of grace on your head and present you with a crown of splendor." Women are the source of wisdom, and wisdom is "supreme." Therefore women are supreme.

When God speaks to a couple, He speaks to the wife first. For instance, when Jesus was conceived, the angel Gabriel approached Mary first (see Luke 1:26-38). And God followed this pattern at His resurrection when the angels announced Jesus' resurrection to the women first (see Luke 24:1-12). Because the conception of Christ and His resurrection are two of the most important moments in Christian history, we can use this principle in less important issues.

The apostle Paul underscores the value of women over men: "I will therefore that the younger women marry, bear children, guide the house, give none occasion to the adversary to speak reproachfully" (1 Timothy 5:14 KJV). According to *Strong's Exhaustive Concordance of the Word of God,* the root word for "guide the house" means "head of the household."[2]

As for husbands, Proverbs 31 clearly commands them to sit at the city gate (verse 23). So Christian husbands need to be away from the home and let their wives be in charge. If men aren't sitting at the city gates, they're in direct violation of God's ordained roles.

I could write reams in this vein, and there are many more references that pour through my mind. But I'm sure I've proven my point. You're either chuckling at how ridiculous this sounds or you're astounded that anyone would use the Bible in this manner. You might even be flabbergasted that I twisted Scripture this way. But in many subtle ways, the "traditional" church has taught in this vein for generations...except placing men over women in God's eyes and in the human value scale.

The surprising fact is that many times women support it as much as the men do because they were taught this way from birth and honestly believe it's truth. The results have been devastating to women, men, and their marriages. While gender prejudices put the object of the prejudice into bondage, they also chain the one who holds the prejudice. Marriages then fall apart.

Unfortunately sometimes the churches that work to save marriages actually splinter them with the concepts they present. Oddly, many people in the church believe that the best way to battle men-hating, radical feminism is to embrace yesterday's cultural male chauvinism. They insist that if a woman doesn't embrace this mindset she must be a feminist, which is condemned by many in traditional Christian circles. But whether the Bible is used to prove that men rule or women rule, *both* stances are unbalanced and *both* desecrate most of what Jesus Christ said and taught.

In his book *Healing for Damaged Emotions,* David Seamands speaks of a survey of Christian women conveyed by Christian psychologist James Dobson. In this survey "Dr. Dobson listed ten sources of depression. He asked the women to number them in the order of how they affected their lives...What came out way ahead of the others? Low self-esteem. Fifty percent of these women rated it first; 80 percent rated it in the top two or three...These women were battling depression that came chiefly from the downward pull of feelings of low self-worth."[3]

A significant reason many Christian women suffer from low self-esteem is because some churches use the Word of God in a way that convinces women they really are of lesser worth. Seamands further asks, "Can you see the wasted emotional and spiritual potential?"[4] The tragedy is that there is a sea of Christian women who *have* wasted their emotional and spiritual potential because they've been told from birth they just don't matter as much as men.

When Christian women are taught this all or most of their lives, they fall into "self-fulfilling prophecy." According to Judy Pearson and Paul Nelson, "The self-fulfilling prophecy is relevant to self-concept. Our concept of ourselves originated in the responses we received when we were young, and, to some extent, self-fulfilling prophecies help to maintain our self-concept. In many ways, we attempt to behave consistently with other peoples' expectations, regardless of whether those expectations are positive or negative."[5] The philosopher René Descartes said it more cryptically, "I think therefore I am." Proverbs 23:7 puts it like this, "As he thinks in his heart, so is he."

Women who are told they are secondary to men fulfill what they've been told. The result? They seldom reach their full potential. According to Elizabeth O'Connor, "In our society, at the age of five, 90 percent of the population measures 'high creativity.' By the age of seven, the figure has dropped to 10 percent. And the percentage of adults with high creativity is only 2 percent! Our creativity is destroyed not through the use of outside force, but through criticism, innuendo, subtle psychological means which the 'well-trained' child learns to use upon [herself or] himself! Most of us are our own 'brain police.' "[6]

A dispute arose among [the disciples] as to which of them was considered to be greatest. Jesus said to them, "The kings of the Gentiles lord it over them; and those who exercise authority over them call themselves Benefactors. But you are not to be like that. Instead, the greatest among you should be like the youngest, and the one who rules like the one who serves. For who is greater, the one who is at the table or the one who serves? Is it not the one who is at the table? But I am among you as one who serves."

LUKE 22:24-26

When it comes to women, some churches have encouraged them to be their own "brain police" in the name of holding up traditional "biblical truth." I believe many women turn from God's call, rejecting His inner promptings to step forward, because they question the call since it seems to contradict what they've been taught about their roles. This often involves pouring active, creative, and vital energies into the romance and sexuality of their marriages. Because they've been taught that's their husband's God-ordained role, they do nothing while their husbands lie awake at night and long for wives who would dare to knock their socks off.

Genesis 1:27 clearly states that both men and women are created in the image of God. When we demean, despise, or disempower the opposite sex, we are dishonoring God.

In a close observation of Jesus' treatment of both men and women, He gave them equal respect. Considering the men in that society viewed most women as inconsequential, or even as dogs, and that women had few or no rights, this was flabbergasting to the disciples. When Christ had a conversation with the woman at the well, the disciples were shocked. Jewish teachers simply did not talk to women in public. Not only did Jesus converse with a woman, but also a *Samaritan* woman, whom the Jews despised due to racial issues. Notice that the disciples didn't question His actions. I think by this point Jesus had told them they were "dull" so many times they didn't want that diagnosis again.

Ultimately, prejudices can destroy your chances of having an exciting, uninhibited marriage. The power of a blazing love affair marriage is so great that it blows the mind, but it can only happen when partners value and respect each other.

Tragically, many couples who embrace gender prejudices as the basis for their marriages spend their lives just having sex, and sometimes very dull sex indeed. These people never experience the explosive and magnetic nature of a thriving love affair.

When Jesus is the tie that binds, he rules, nobody drools.

Prayer Points

* Ask God to show you any prejudices you have embraced as truth.
* If He shows you any, pray daily that God will deliver you and renew your mind. Make a conscious effort to retrain your mind. Without regular prayer on the subject, prejudices engrained over a lifetime may reemerge.
* Ask God to help you encounter Scripture afresh.
* If you have children, be still before the Lord and ask Him to show you how to unravel any prejudices that have been woven into them.
* Pray that God will give you patience with your mate if he or she doesn't see or admit the existence of gender prejudices.

Love and Romance

Celebrate your mate's gender by joining him or her in doing something that he or she typically likes to do with same-sex friends. For instance, if your wife enjoys window shopping, dedicate a day to window shopping with her. (Wear comfortable shoes!) Let her know you appreciate her femininity by complimenting her. Tell her she's beautiful to you. If your husband loves to hunt, put on camouflage and sit in that deer stand with him. (Remember, no perfume and don't wear clothes washed in scented detergent.) Tell him how much you respect his strength. Even after 28 years of marriage, my husband loves it when I make a big deal about his muscles.

"In a love-base marriage, thoughts of one mate
subordinating the other are detestable."

Leading and Following

*Do not be called leaders; for One is your Leader,
that is, Christ. But the greatest among you shall
be your servant. Whoever exalts himself shall be humbled;
and whoever humbles himself shall be exalted.*

MATTHEW 23:10-12 NASB

In 2005 Daniel and I had been praying for about a year that God would provide another home for us that included plenty of space for our growing ministry. The ministry had taken over our living area. We were in a holding tank with trails throughout. Boxes of books cluttered every available space. Our music equipment added to the mix, while the suitcases from the last trip were sitting here and there.

We live in a small town in east Texas that doesn't provide a lot of options for reasonably priced ministry headquarters. Okay, to put it bluntly, chances of finding what we needed in our town were zero. Every existing home we looked at would have to be adapted to our needs, which meant spending even more money on top of the original price tag. And the price tag on what we needed wasn't cheap. We also needed more in a ministry headquarters site than our budget permitted.

We prayed for God to provide what we needed. After looking, I prayed that the Lord would open the door of the ministry site He wanted to give us. At that point, one of the places we had looked at began to rotate through my mind. It was a large, older home with a 2,000-square foot building beside it, along with more than six acres, a pond, a monster-sized pool, a baseball field, a tennis/basketball court, and a volleyball court. It had been on the market for two years with no offers. Because of its condition, the owner was selling for a price that fit our budget, but we'd have to spend so much in renovations that there was no way we could afford it.

Daniel and I both dismissed the home, but God kept bringing it back to my mind. Finally I told Daniel I felt we should look at the place again and make an offer. Daniel was skeptical, but he agreed. We went to look and saw even more work than we'd originally noticed. The house had six layers of roofing that dated back to the 1930s!

Daniel said, "The most we can pay is half what he's asking."

I e-mailed the real estate agent and told her the most we'd offer was half the asking price because of all the remodeling that needed to be done. I didn't realize we were making an "official offer." But the agent e-mailed the owner with our price. And he said we had a deal!

Now, considering neither Daniel nor I understood we were making an official offer, this totally surprised us. We wandered around our house for a few days staring into space and saying, "Now what do we do?" I soon realized that God was beating us over the head, saying, "Hello! Buy it! Buy it now!"

I said, "Daniel, I think we should buy it." Although I was convinced the home purchase was God's will, I didn't push Daniel into agreeing with me. I waited for him to come to his own comfort zone with God over it. And he would have done the exact same thing with me.

In retrospect, I believe God used both Daniel and me at crucial times in giving us this home and ministry site. The Lord kept bringing the home to my mind and impressed me to tell Daniel that we should look at the place again and make an offer. He used Daniel in knowing how much to offer. I was as convinced we should take another look as Daniel was that we shouldn't pay any more than half what the guy was asking. We respected each other enough to go along with what the other felt so strongly about.

During our home purchase, neither one of us followed the other, and no one was given the final say. We worked together to honor God's guidance until we agreed on what to do. This is how we make all our joint decisions, and the way we approach every area of our marriage, spirituality, and home. Because we don't impose limitations on ourselves or God, He is free to work through both of us in fulfilling His perfect will in our lives and our home.

Jesus Christ and Noah Webster

And when we think we lead, we are most led.

LORD BYRON

In the Christian world, there's a lot of talk about leadership. In regard to marriage, the most popular stance for many years has been the husband is to lead the family and wife in all things and specifically be the spiritual leader for the family. Interestingly enough, in Matthew 23:10-12 Jesus Christ says, "Do not be called leaders." Notice Jesus didn't say, "Don't take positions of leadership or influence." He said, "Do not be *called* leaders." To paraphrase this passage, Jesus said, "Don't think of yourself in terms of others following you. There's one you all should follow—Christ. He is your leader. Instead of focusing on who's following you, focus on having a servant's heart and encouraging others to follow Christ—not you—by your example." If we are to use Christ's teachings as the basis for our marriages, we must seriously grapple with how His statement impacts the issue of leadership in marriage.

First, let's start with a definition of leadership. There are two basic definitions at play here. Jesus defined leadership as servanthood. (He turned so many human instincts inside out!) "But many who are first will be last, and many who are last will be first" (Matthew 19:30) and "whoever finds his life will lose it, and whoever loses his life for my sake will find it" (Matthew 10:39). These are radical ideas. So when Christ defined leadership as servanthood and nothing else, He was staying in the context of His general message.

When the word "leader" is used around the church or as it applies to marriage, Christ's definition is lost or diluted. Instead, our culture's definition of leadership, as detailed by Noah Webster, is used: "A person who leads...a guide...A person who has commanding authority."[1] He defines leadership as "the office or position of a leader...the act or an instance of leading."[2]

There are many churchgoers who have a fit if anyone suggests a wife can or should "lead" her husband or family. They are adamant that leadership is for husbands. But the same people are perfectly fine with the suggestion that wives should *serve* their husbands and families. Ironically, whether it's the husband or wife thinking the spouse should follow or that he or she holds first place, *both* views are out of alignment with the teachings of Christ.

In discussing this definition of leadership, Joseph Coleson calls it a "non-Christian, anti-Christian model of leadership/followership, one that Jesus himself specifically condemned" (see Mark 10:42-45; John 12:25-26).[3] Jesus' paraphrased words based on Matthew 10:39 state the same: "Don't even think of yourselves as the one everyone else follows...the one up front or in first place." Note: Jesus was talking to his 12 male disciples when He said this.

Shouldn't husbands and wives *both* exhibit Christ's definition of leadership in their homes and for each other? Shouldn't *both* spouses strive to be Christlike and pour themselves out for each other in unconditional service and love? The true issue isn't who leads and who follows. The crux is how closely *both* spouses are willing to align their hearts and minds with the heart and mind of Christ.

Are we willing to stop using the Bible to defend and support yesterday's cultural traditions long enough to discover God's intended design for marriages? Are we willing to allow the words of Christ to be the source of our definitions, and then shape our marriages based on His model? How willing are we to approach everything the apostle Paul wrote about marriage and view it in context of what Jesus taught and did?

Jesus Christ and the Apostle Paul

As demonstrated in chapter 2, one problem is that too often we decide what we want to teach about marriage *and then* go to the Word of God to back us up. Many Bible scholars call this "proof texting." Others call it "strip-mining the Word of God." We have a choice in approaching the Word of God: We can either prove our point while ignoring anything that contradicts it or we can face the seeming contradictions head-on and create a method of evaluation that brings agreement and balance to the concepts we find.

There are numerous passages in which Paul implies that wives are subordinated to their husbands and that husbands should think of themselves in first place and their wives in second place—in God's eyes as well as in the eyes of the church. Several hundred years ago these key passages were used to give men license to treat their wives in any way they chose, including spanking, beating, rape, and verbal abuse. Most people back then would have been shocked and outraged if this belief was challenged openly. A few of these verses from Paul include:

> That they [aged women] may teach the young women to be sober, to love their husbands [NIV: be "subject to their husbands"], to love their children, to be discreet, chaste, keepers at home, good, obedient to their own husbands, that the word of God be not blasphemed (Titus 2:4-5 KJV).

> Wives, submit to your husbands as to the Lord. For the husband is the head of the wife as Christ is the head of the church, his body, of which he is the Savior. Now as the church submits to Christ, so also wives should submit to their husbands in everything (Ephesians 5:22-24).

> Now I want you to realize that the head of every man is Christ, and the head of the woman is man, and the head of Christ is God...A man ought not to cover his head, since he is the image and glory of God; but the woman is the glory of man. For man did not come from woman, but woman from man; neither was man created for woman, but woman for man (1 Corinthians 11:3,7-8).

> As in all congregations of the saints, women should remain silent in the

churches. They are not allowed to speak, but must be in submission, as the Law says. If they want to inquire about something, they should ask their own husbands at home; for it is disgraceful for a woman to speak in church (1 Corinthians 14:33-35).

A woman should learn in quietness and full submission. I do not permit a woman to teach or to have authority over a man; she must be silent (1 Timothy 2:11).

Over the decades the way these verses have been interpreted has changed, gradually becoming less severe. Nevertheless, the Bible is still "strip-mined" to promote, at the very least, Webster's definition of leadership while ignoring Jesus' leadership. So wives are taught they are to walk behind their husbands and at the same time told they are equally valuable to their husbands. This gives lip service to the current cultural norm of equal value between husband and wife. Furthermore, the traditional Christian marriage is still taught as a hierarchy, which is what Christ said not to think in terms of.

It's understandable that so many in the church cling to the hierarchical form of marriage and view of gender relations because a surface read of these verses out of the context of Paul and Jesus' total statements does seem to support the wife walking a step—or a mile—behind the husband in all areas of the home and marriage, including her spirituality. A literal interpretation of some of these verses would mean that women and wives are to be mute in their marriages, homes, and churches. And partially or totally mute wives often create women who are enablers, which is contrary to the actions of Christ.

However, remember Paul's statement in 2 Corinthians 10: "You are looking only on the surface of things. If anyone is confident that he belongs to Christ, he should consider again that we belong to Christ just as much as he" (verse 7).

Whatever Paul meant when he said that wives are to obey or be subject to their husbands in all things, he also said both husbands and wives are to submit or be subject to each other (Ephesians 5:21).

Whatever Paul meant when he said the husband is the head of the wife, he also used the root word for head of the household in referring to young women getting married and managing their homes (1 Timothy 5:14).

Whatever Paul meant when he said the head of every woman is man, he also said the head of Christ is God. Since we believe as Christians that God the Father and God the Son are equally one with the Holy Spirit, the word "head" cannot be interpreted in a hierarchical context. Paul immediately supports this when he states that men and women both depend on each other and both come from God, which strongly implies equality, not one-upmanship. (See 1 Corinthians 11:11-12.)

Whatever Paul meant when he said women were to be silent in the church, he also commended women who *weren't* silent in the church or were active in his ministry. "Greet Priscilla and Aquila [wife and husband, respectively], my fellow workers in Christ Jesus. They risked their lives for me. Not only I but all the churches of the Gentiles are grateful to them. Greet also the church that meets at their house" (Romans 16:3-5). "I commend to you our sister Phoebe, a servant of the church in Cenchrea. I ask you to receive her in the Lord in a way worthy of the saints and to give her any help she may need from you, for she has been a great help to many people, including me" (Romans 16:1-2). According to the *Reflecting God Study Bible's* note on this passage, " 'Servants' [means] one who serves or ministers in any way. When church related, as it is here, it probably refers to a specific office—woman deacon or deaconess."[4]

Whatever Paul meant when he said that a woman should not be in authority over a man, Jesus Christ said to his male disciples, "Neither be ye called masters [NIV: teacher]: for one is your Master [NIV: Teacher], even Christ" (Matthew 23:10 KJV). Instead He advised them to "humble yourself and become like a child." An argument started among the disciples as to which of them would be the greatest. Jesus, knowing their thoughts, took a little child and had him stand beside him. Then he said to them, 'Whoever welcomes this little child in my name welcomes me; and whoever welcomes me welcomes the one who sent me. For he who is least among you all—he is the greatest'" (Luke 9:46-48).

Also in regard to Paul's stating that women should not teach or be in authority over men, many noted scholars suggest that we take into account the cultural ramifications that were at play when Paul wrote these passages. Most women were illiterate and, therefore, limited by lack of knowledge and training.

And behind every man who's a failure there's a woman, too!

JOHN RUGE

Most Christians do take into account cultural issues on many other topics. For instance, most believers don't use the Bible to validate the Old Testament practice of polygamy, even though many of the beloved and applauded patriarchs had more than one wife. Instead, we recognize and accept that polygamy was a cultural norm that is counter to God's overall plan for marriages. Likewise, Christians don't endorse stoning a rebellious child. Most understand that the Old Testament practice of stoning rebels should be left in that old time.

In regard to the New Testament passages in question, whether the cultural issues are accepted as viable or not, whatever Paul meant shouldn't be interpreted in a way that contradicts anything Jesus said. Paul was in alignment with Jesus' teaching when he said women shouldn't think of themselves in authority over men because Jesus Christ repeatedly made general statements on this level to men as well, telling them not to call themselves masters, leaders, or teachers. Whatever positions men or women hold in church, they are not supposed to think of themselves as "large and in charge," using the position to empower the self or think of themselves as "more elevated" or "more important" than another. Instead, they are to embrace their positions as opportunities to serve and empower others, just as Jesus served and empowered.

Over and over again Jesus basically said, "Don't even think of yourselves as one rung higher than another person. Become like a child. Become a servant." And Paul said, "For by the grace given me I say to every one of you: Do not think of yourself more highly than you ought, but rather think of yourself with sober judgment, in accordance with the measure of faith God has given you" (Romans 12:3). He further stated, "Do nothing out of selfish ambition or vain conceit, but in humility consider others better than yourselves. Each of you should look not only to your own interests, but also to the interests of others" (Philippians 2:3-4).

Spiritual Growth and Disillusionment

There are many Christian women who are disillusioned with their husbands' spiritual leadership. These women have been told, some practically since birth, that their husbands should possess more spiritual knowledge and depth than they do. Women have been taught that husbands should lead (Webster dictionary style) in all matters.

In their book *TeamMates*, Bob and Yvonne Turnball state that they have had such reports for years from women throughout the United States and Canada. Many of these women are disillusioned with their husbands because the husbands don't give them spiritual [Webster] leadership in all areas.[5] They've been told over and over that they are to follow their husbands' lead and, often, to not initiate, even in their areas of expertise. At best this is frustrating when a woman is deeper spiritually in some areas than her husband. At worst it causes a woman to become spiritually stunted because she's not growing spiritually for fear of violating her assigned role. However, Paul said, "Therefore, my dear friends, as you have always obeyed—not only in my presence, but now much more in my absence—continue to work out your salvation with fear and trembling, for it is God who works in you to will and to act according to his good purpose" (Philippians 2:12-13). This letter was written to both men and women...husbands and wives. We are each supposed to work out our own salvation.

Nonetheless, some women—a minority though—have been convinced they should view their husbands as god-like figures whom they should obey, even if what they're told contradicts the Word of God. (I watched a church-sponsored video series that supports this view.) These extreme cases lead women astray.

After traveling the United States for years and listening to thousands of women in numerous denominations, I've come to the conclusion that some women *want* their husbands to be their "gods." They believe it's much easier to view their spouses as their gods and just do what they say and place their spiritual well-being on the men's shoulders than take responsibility for their own walks with God and devote serious time to developing intimacy with Christ and allowing His mind to become theirs. According to David Seamands, "Many married people fail to allow God to do for them what only God can do. Then they ask other human beings, their spouses, to do what they cannot possibly do. If they work at it, men make good husbands, and women make good wives. But they make lousy gods. They're not meant for that."[6]

In the Old Testament, the Children of Israel came to a point where they demanded a king. "Give us a king!" they declared, and God answered with, "But I want to be your king" (1 Samuel 8). But the Children of Israel continued to demand a king, and God complied. Sometimes I wonder if God is saying the same thing to us about our homes. Maybe some women want a human hierarchy– a king or ruler– and the whole time God is saying, "But I want to be your king. I want to be on the throne of your home. I want to be the one you *both* look to." This is called theocracy and is what Adam and Eve experienced in the Garden of Eden before sin entered their hearts.

Sometimes the men who are exhibiting Jesus' leadership the most in their homes are the ones whose wives are the most disenchanted. While the husbands are fulfilling the teachings of Jesus Christ in serving, sacrificing, and empowering their families, the women are expecting them to exhibit Webster's definition of leadership and be a step ahead of them in all areas of growth. When women have been taught a cultural-based definition of leadership rather than a Christ-based one, they expect a human king.

From this error, many women believe their husbands have failed them. They gradually become disheartened with their mates and their marriages. They begin looking at other men who seem to "show [Webster] spiritual leadership" more than their husbands. Temptations can and do set in. Most areas of the marriage are affected, including sexuality.

I don't think any Christian man or woman who truly loves the Lord would purposefully choose to adopt concepts that hinder marriage. Problems usually fall more under the category of repeating what has been taught without thinking through the sources or ramifications. The tragedy is that the men who do insist their wives follow them spiritually, or in any other vein, are usually married to earnest women who desperately want to obey the Lord. So these women follow a step behind their husbands. They follow right into the bedroom, and when they land in bed they don't do a whole lot of anything there except follow or respond. And if they're fully disillusioned with their husbands, they might not do much responding. This does not encourage blazing marital love. In fact, it often squashes it!

Many husbands then choose to have mistresses, whom they never tell to follow them. And those mistresses put way more energy into sex than the wives ever did...and husbands are dazzled past logic. From there a husband may leave his wife and family and devote himself to the mistress. Ironically, if he marries the mistress and applies the same subordination role to her that he did to his previous wife, the mistress will eventually stop responding in bed as well.

Prayer Points

* Ask the Lord to give you a clear vision of what leadership means to Him.

* If you are female, pray that God will show you if you are subconsciously wanting your husband to be your god or if you have emotional issues that fuel a desire for your husband to rule you.

* If you are male, ask the Lord to equip you to fully align your thinking and the patterns of your marriage with Christ's definitions of leadership.

* Wait before the Lord and be willing to be the instruments of His heart.

* Meditate on the difference between passivity and active servanthood. Pray that God will empower you to be an active servant.

Love and Romance

Wherever you go together, walk side-by-side if possible. It's very easy for one spouse to outpace the other. Think about slowing down or speeding up to stay in stride with your mate. Offer to help each other if something is being carried. If hands are free, hold hands or walk arm-in-arm. Smile into your mate's eyes. Let the world know you're joint heirs, partners in Christ.

> "In a loved-based marriage, leadership is
> defined as servanthood and both
> spouses lavishly serve the other."

Healthy Balance

There is neither Jew nor Greek, slave nor free,
male nor female, for you are all one in Christ Jesus.

GALATIANS 3:28

T his past Mother's Day was my best ever. My husband ordered a corsage from the florist. To me that means he actually *planned* to get me a corsage. He didn't wait until the last minute and rush to the department store. Then Daniel took the kids shopping, and they bought me a digital photo frame, which scrolls through digital photos from a memory stick and displays them on the screen. This way I can continually see many of the photos I've had on file for years. Daniel and the kids also took me out to eat. All this happened on the Friday and Saturday before Mother's Day. I thought that was all they'd prepared for me.

On Sunday morning Daniel brought the tape player to our room and said, "Here's our last gift for you. I want you to listen to what the kids and I have to say. I was speechless as "Have I Told You Lately That I Love You" by Rod Stewart played in the background while both my children told me how much they appreciated and loved me. A big subject with both of them was the fact that I am always there to help with school and homework, to go on field trips with them, and to attend their class parties. My son cried through his expression of appreciation for my being there for him. My daughter's sweet voice reminded me of how thankful she was that we sacrificed to get her from Vietnam.

I wept through the whole tape.

Then Daniel's voice came on, and his message was quite different from Brett and Brooke's. He said,

Now, Debra, I'd like to say that I love you today more than I ever have before. And I'm very, very thankful that God has allowed us to have many wonderful years together. You truly are my best friend. You're a wonderful wife and a phenomenal mother to Brett and Brooke. And I'm very, very blessed to have you as my wife and the mother of our children.

The book of Proverbs talks about a virtuous woman. And that's what I believe you are, Debra. You have all the characteristics of the lady talked about and described. You praise your family and praise your husband, and you lift us up. And you do things for us and you sacrifice your love for us unconditionally. And I want to let you know that's truly how I feel about you—what the book of Proverbs says. I haven't told you that enough in the past, but I want you to know today that I believe that.

And I believe with all my heart that that's the kind of woman you are. So we want to honor you today, and we want to say Happy Mother's Day to you. And I want to thank you for some things you've done in our lives and thank you for some things you've done for me personally.

I want to thank you for sharing your experiences and lessons that life has taught you. And I want to thank you for things you've helped me overcome. You read books and study the Bible and you commune with God. You travel all over the USA, and you share insights and knowledge. It helps transform many people's lives.

And you're a wonderful blessing to a lot of people, but while doing that—that has rubbed off on us and you've impacted our lives greatly and you've helped me rise up out of a lot of emotional baggage and emotional issues, and you've helped me come out of it all. I'm a different man today than I was when we got married—a better man. A whole lot of that is due to you, Debra. And I want to thank you for that, and I want to thank you for everything you've done for us as a family.

So with all that said we want to dedicate a song to you because we do thank you and we love you. This song has a lot of the things that the writer of the song talks about that you do. And I believe that one day this will be a picture of you in heaven. For now we want you to sit back and listen to the song and realize that when we hear it, we think of you and we believe that this is you.

So here's the song. Hope you enjoy it and hope you have a wonderful day.

I then sat and listened through Ray Boltz singing "Thank You for Giving to the Lord." I cried some more and could only hope that I lived up to all the things Daniel and the kids said. Even though I try with all my heart, I fail at times. At the very end of that song, Daniel's voice came on again. "Thank you, Debra. Thank you for being my wife and for loving me unconditionally. Thank you for being the mother of Brett and Brooke and for being the foundation and the spirit of our home. We thank you and hope you enjoy the day. Happy Mother's Day. We love you."

All adult Christians are held equally accountable for their behaviors and responses.[1]

ROBERT HICKS

When Webster's Definition Agrees with Jesus'

In the previous chapter we saw that many Christians define leadership by Webster's dictionary's definition of leader—the person who is in first place. Because of this, many churches reference a few Scriptures to support that the husband is supposed to teach and lead the wife spiritually, and the wife is not supposed to teach or give insights to the husband. The Scripture most often pulled out to prove this is Titus 2:5, which states that wives are to "be subject to their husbands." From this one verse, many churches teach that husbands are supposed to initiate everything from communication to spirituality, regardless of their wives' gifts. I've heard a few pastors tell wives that if they sin because their husbands tell them to, God will not hold them accountable. Unbelievable...and unscriptural!

This narrow view of Scripture and marriage creates an inconsistent interpretation of human behavior. For instance, when wives ask questions about spiritual issues at church, I've personally heard men say women "want male leadership," and that their husbands must be failing to give them leadership at home. Consequently, the wives have to turn to other men in the church. However, when husbands ask the same people similar questions, the husbands are applauded for "exhibiting strong leadership" in wanting to grow. Could it be that in *both* cases, regardless of gender, the person with the questions simply wants to learn more of God and grow in Him?

I get numerous e-mails and phone calls from husbands with questions about their marriages. This doesn't mean their wives aren't giving them "female leadership" and so they are turning to another female. It just means they have problems, they need answers, they're connecting with someone who can help.

I recall a heated e-mail I received a few years ago from a lady who sounded like she was ready to explode. She believed husbands were never supposed to learn anything from wives. Wives were supposed to learn from husbands. She was basing her belief on a few isolated Scriptures and ignoring common sense, as well as other Scriptures that contradicted her theory.

The poor woman admitted her marriage was as dysfunctional as all get out. But she was determined to "honor God's call as a wife" and silently sit in the dysfunction until her husband "woke up" and realized she was supposed to learn from him. Her silence was only entrenching the dysfunction. She didn't mention their sex life, but given similar stories I've encountered and the significant issues she detailed, I imagine their bedroom life could put a tornado in neutral.

Webster's dictionary does offer one definition of "lead" that can complement the teachings of Christ: "to show (someone) the way to go by accompanying him."[2] This definition in no way implies that one person is following the other. Rather, it suggests coming alongside and accompanying each other.

When a husband and wife get married, they each bring to the union life experiences—some good, some bad. If they are Christians, they also bring differing levels of spiritual growth and insights in various areas and subjects. In the healthiest marriages, both the husband and wife are free to share these insights with each other and, thus, encourage growth. After a few years as a team, the husband and wife have essentially combined their strengths and growth to make a stronger whole. As the years continue to rock on, if they both seek the Lord and grow in His grace, they will both continue to learn new insights and wisdom they can share with each other.

When Daniel and I married we both had enough emotional issues and baggage and dysfunctional coping mechanisms to destroy more than one marriage. Neither one of us ever had an affair or physically abused the other, but our problems were severely destructive to our relationship. After a few years of marriage, I began seriously seeking deliverance and studying Christian psychology books for help and healing. Daniel will tell you that he was in denial of needing any help. But I knew we both desperately needed it. So I kept studying and kept growing and kept talking about the concepts I learned. Eventually, he realized he and I both direly needed emotional deliverance. And with both of us open to the Holy Spirit's healing balm, God began to unfold a miracle in our hearts and lives.

In the case of our healing and deliverance, if I had adopted the teaching that a husband was supposed to always lead the wife and he was not supposed to be taught by a woman, Daniel and I would still be stuck in dysfunction. In fact, I fully believe that without God's deliverance, we would probably be divorced.

Once the healing began, I learned from Daniel and he learned from me. We came alongside each other and taught each other what God was showing us. We blended the best of who we were while allowing God to remove the scars and ugliness. And that made a greater whole.

With all that said, I've never met another man who exhibits "Christ leadership" more than my husband. I view him as much the foundation of our home as he views me. After a very stormy first decade in our marriage, he has grown into an amazing husband and father. If ever there was a living testimony to God's performing a miracle in a relationship, we are it. Daniel pours himself out for the kids and me. He uses his masculine strength to protect us and our home. He keeps his word. I never have to worry about his showing up when he says he's going to be somewhere. I also don't doubt that he would drop everything and come to my aid at any time for any reason.

What sets our marriage apart from many is that I do the exact same thing for Daniel. I'm living Christ in our home and marriage just as strongly as my husband is. God's miraculous healing needed to impact my heart and emotions as much as it did Daniel's, and it has. While I don't physically protect my husband, I use the power of my femininity to *sexually* protect him because "[Love] always protects" (1 Corinthians 13:7). I pour myself out for our kids and him. I keep my word. If he needs me, I'm there. He never doubts that I'll be at his side if he calls on me.

We don't view being Christlike as role specific. We don't view church attendance, Bible study, prayer, and spiritual growth as role specific. In order to view any of these as role specific, we would have to believe that Christ's general commands, such as, "If anyone would come after me, he must deny himself and take up his cross and follow me" (Matthew 16:24), apply to men only. But we don't believe that. So we both pray with our children and teach them and take equal responsibility in keeping the family in church. We view the kids' spiritual development as our joint responsibility.

Many say that the current societal roles have changed and that women are now taking a more active part in the spirituality of their homes and families than husbands, and that's a reversal of the way it should be. This is based on the assumption that yesterday's cultural patterns represented God's will. But really, it's just as unbalanced when husbands pour all or most of their energy into the family and wives pour little or none. Neither spouse should be wholly responsible for the spirituality of the family, church attendance, and the condition of the marriage. In the healthiest marriages and homes, both spouses share the responsibilities. The spouses are true partners.

That's what Daniel and I are. We aren't basing our marriage on cultural norms from yesterday or today, but on the heart of Christ. Neither one of us expects the other to follow. Instead, we walk side-by-side, arm-in-arm.

Ministry, Word, and the World

I'm not saying or even implying that fathers and husbands shouldn't bravely answer God's call to impact society and their homes. If ever there was a time in history when we need strong men of God to be strong men of God, it is now! We need courageous men in politics and law, family ministries, and the home. We need husbands who will be loyal and true and upright and holy. We need men who will walk the straight and narrow and avoid sexual perversion.

I am immensely thankful for many national ministries that promote the gospel and stand in the gap to bring people to God. I am grateful for ministries and denominations that promote balanced biblical scholarship that encourages both genders to be all they can be for Christ. Because, truly, we also need an army of wives and women who will answer God's call as well. We need brave women who will stand against Satan's attacks and become spiritual prayer warriors. We need women who will set holy standards for their families and our culture and speak up when those standards are violated. We need women who are courageous enough to accept God's call even if they are ridiculed for it.

I have repeatedly heard teaching that the only reason a woman ever feels God's call is because there was a man God called first and he rejected the call. There is no Scripture to back this theory. It is based on the erroneous belief that God calls and equips men first and women only as backups. This implies that women are secondary; that in God's eyes men come first or are better. As already mentioned, there are many situations in the Bible where women were called before men—just as there are many situations in the Bible where men were called before women.

Countless preachers, Christian leaders, and teachers have said that when men will be all that God has called them to be, our nation, homes, and marriages will be transformed. I fully agree that when men of God fully commit their lives wholly to Christ and set their goals on pleasing Him wonderful changes will take place. And I'm thankful for groups that encourage men to be all God means for them to be.

However, for these radical changes to occur women also need to be all God calls them to be. If only one gender turns into saints, conflicts in the world and in our nation won't go away. Men *and* women both need to be encouraged to fully commit their lives to Christ and live accordingly. And in a marriage, when both husband and wife are fully Christ-centered, breathtaking, miraculous things happen. The well-being of our homes, marriages, nation, and world rests on the shoulders of both men and women.

Each bears an equal responsibility that is desperately needed.

Each is called of God to develop intimacy with Him.

Each carries a powerful impact that the other cannot replace.

Neither should neglect the marriage, home, or children in favor of career or ministry.

Tragically, when women of God are taught that their role is to give lesser input or to be passive and quiet in their marriages or to wait on their husbands to possess the knowledge and skills for "Webster" leading in all occasions, then often homes and marriages greatly suffer or fall apart. And it would be the same if the "role" was reversed and husbands were taught to be passive and quiet. It's as impossible to conceive a healthy home spiritually and a healthy marriage in all areas with the husband's input alone as it is to conceive a child with the husband's input alone. As neither the male nor female element in the conception of the child is more important than the other, neither is the husband's nor wife's input into the marriage and home more important than the other.

There is no passage in the Bible that tells women to limit or discontinue the manifestation of their spiritual gifts and insights in their homes and marriages. Concepts built with such a thrust are limiting God's work and plan!

Balancing Paul

As mentioned in the previous chapter, even though the apostle Paul made some strong statements about mutuality in marriage and gender relations, he also made some stark statements that seem to imply the hierarchical approach to marriage and gender relations. But Jesus Christ repeatedly denounced hierarchical thinking. Since Christians fully believe the Word of God is divinely inspired, one section can't contradict another.

When approaching the passages where Paul's "hierarchical" statements seemingly contradict his other teachings and the teachings of Christ, it's important to develop a method that doesn't compromise truth or violate Jesus' emphasis on servanthood and not elevating the self. Since the Bible makes at least as many references to the power and influence of women as to men, it is reasonable to realize that both husbands and wives influence and come alongside to guide

> *My personal view is that both [husband and wife] have authority in the home and each must be willing to give up that authority in order to achieve mutual submission and love.*[3]
>
> ROBERT HICKS

each other through life. Scripture so aptly describes this in relation to friends: "Two are better than one, because they have a good return for their work: If one falls down, his friend can help him up. But pity the man who falls and has no one to help him up!" (Ecclesiastes 4:9-11). Genesis 2:18 says something similar of the husband and wife: "The LORD God said, "It is not good for the man to be alone. I will make a helper suitable for him." According to the *Reflecting God Study Bible,* "For the first time in creation something is 'not good.' Without female companionship and a partner in reproduction, the man could not fully realize his humanity. 'Helper' does not imply subordination; indeed, it is often used of God Himself (Psalm 33:20; 70:5; 121:2)."[4] According to noted theologian Joseph Coleson, the word "helper" means "a power like him, facing him as equal."[5] However, as already stated, Christ never called anyone to strive for equality, but rather to have a servant's heart.

When Paul wrote, "For the husband is the head of the wife as Christ is the head of the church" (Ephesians 5:23) and "the head of the woman is man" (1 Corinthians 11:3), the most logical and balanced interpretation of the word "head" is "fountainhead of life" or "source," as defined by Lawrence Richards in his *Bible Background Commentary: New Testament*.[6] Paul echoes this truth in 1 Corinthians in the verses that come after the use of the word "head": "In the Lord, however, woman is not independent of man, nor is man independent of woman. For as woman came from man, so also man is born of woman. But everything comes from God" (11:11-12). When Paul uses the turn of phrase "in the Lord, however," he is specifically stating that being "in the Lord" makes a difference, or *should* make a difference, in gender relations. By interpreting "head" as "source," we get agreement in Paul's complete message: God the Father is the source of God the Son; man is the source of woman, since Eve came from Adam; God is the source of everything.

Furthermore, Richards aptly points out that as Christians we believe the holy trinity is equally one. When Paul says that God is the head of Christ, the apostle is referencing Christ's incarnation; and at Jesus' incarnation His source was God. If we don't interpret "head" as "source" here, we come away believing that God the Son is a subordinated part of the holy trinity, which contradicts Christ's saying, "I and the Father are one" (John 10:30).[7]

According to Brian Nystrom,

> The ideal state of marriage is a reflection of the symbiotic nature and relationship of the Trinity...The Trinity displays co-equality among the three persons, and although there are distinct persons in the Trinity, they are one. The husband–wife partnership displays co-equality between two persons, and though there are two distinct persons in the partnership, they are one. There is a parallel between a Christian-based marriage and the Trinity. In a Christian marriage, both partners are one, both rule together, yet each person is distinct.[8]

Genesis says of Adam and Eve, "They will become one flesh" (2:24). Paul echoes this exact statement in Ephesians 5:31, "For this reason a man will leave his father and mother and be united to his wife, and the two will become one flesh." Viewing a spouse as having more authority than the other actually splinters oneness and compromises the incredible unity, harmony, and emotional intimacy that can occur between husband and wife. Sadly, couples can go their entire marriages and not experience the breathless depths of love and communion that can occur in two hearts that pour themselves out for each other.

Unfortunately, many couples settle for fractured emotional intimacy with an "as good as it gets" mentality. Traditionally, Paul has been used to support this fracturing. And like the homeless in third-world countries drink muddy water and believe it's fine because they've never tasted

> *The sexes were made for each other, and only in the wise and loving union of the two is the fullness of health and duty and happiness to be expected.*
>
> WILLIAM HALL

pure water, many spouses drink of marriage concepts that are far from the pure heart of Christ. Because their parents and grandparents drank the tainted concepts before them, they've never known anything different or seen anything else modeled. So couples believe this is the way marriage is supposed to taste. Yet the words of Jesus forever echo with the essence of a unity these couples have never consumed. Christ can and does give marriages His untainted living water: "If anyone is thirsty, let him come to me and drink. Whoever believes in me, as the Scripture has said, streams of living water will flow from within him" (John 7:37). But spouses must be willing to lift the cup to their lips and fill their souls with its purity.

When spouses don't allow Jesus' living water to permeate their marriages, sexual intimacy is as thwarted as emotional intimacy.

Leadership and Sexuality

Most healthy men don't want a husband-lead/wife-follow relationship when it comes to sex—even the ones who interpret "head" as being the authority. Deep in the hearts of most normal guys, they want their wives to *really want* them sexually and do something about it…something wild and crazy that will leave them dazzled for days. They want wives who are as active in the bedroom as they are and as fun in the shower as they want to be. When it comes to sex, most men want *lovers* who are free to unleash their own sexuality on them, not a subordinate who passively waits for them to initiate sex and then responds without enthusiasm.

When I asked God what to do about my dysfunctional marriage that had very little romance, He spoke to me through Scripture: "So in everything, do to others what you would have them do to you" (Matthew 7:12). God didn't say to wait on my husband to initiate everything. Actually, even though my parents never taught me to always wait on my husband to do everything, without realizing it I had gradually become lulled under the influence of this teaching because so many in the Christian world emphatically teach that this is the wife's God-ordained role. I came to believe that the dynamics of our marriage

> *One-half of knowing what you want is knowing what you must give up before you get it.*
>
> SIDNEY HOWARD

and home were primarily my husband's responsibility. God's scriptural admonishment was like a splash of cold water in my face. I woke up and realized I was buying into something I'd never learned through Scripture. I needed to get with it and do my part in making my marriage sizzle.

As I've noted previously, many Christian wives admit to being disillusioned with their husbands. This is one reason why. They are taught that their husbands are supposed to be more, have more, do more than they are, have, and do—including in the romance department. But the Bible never says this!

"Do to others…" is active, not passive. And when it comes to sex and romance, this means thinking, planning, and sometimes scheming and plotting. And that eventually led my husband and me to lots of fun. I will do the same for you and your spouse!

Prayer Points

* Pray that God will free you from any bondage that is prohibiting you and your mate from sharing the best of who you are with each other.

* Ask God to give you the wisdom to help your mate overcome any emotional or spiritual problems.

* Pray that the Lord will teach you and your mate how to be lovers.

* Ask the Lord to show you how to minister to your mate.

* Be still before the Lord and pray for the courage to do something that will dazzle your mate for weeks.

Love and Romance

Wash your mate's vehicle. Vacuum and clean out the inside too. Leave a sexy note inside that says, "Now that I've washed your vehicle, how about letting me wash you? Join me in the shower (or hot tub or bathtub)." Include a date and time if you wish. Make sure the note is found by your mate only.

In 1 Corinthians 13:5 Paul states, "Love is not self-seeking.'
In a love-based marriage, neither mate uses Scripture
as a tool to elevate the self.

Marriage Paradox

*In this world, it is not what we take up but
what we give up that makes us rich.*

HENRY WARD BEECHER

After we closed the loan on our home and ministry headquarters, the remodeling began. Daniel took charge of his areas of expertise, and I took charge of mine. All the structural issues belonged to Daniel, and the decorating issues were mine. We never had an "official meeting" over this division of responsibility, we just naturally and smoothly fell into it.

The six layers of shingles on the roof had to be removed and replaced. Daniel worked with the contractor to decide what kind of shingles to use. I don't have a clue what shingles are up there and really don't care. I trusted Daniel to figure it out. On every major decision, he'd come to me for input. Most of the time, I'd look at him and say, "That's *your* area of expertise. Do what you think is best."

When it came time to choose the interior paint, that chore was placed on my shoulders. Unlike Daniel and the structural issues, I didn't have one clue what I was doing in choosing the paint. I'd never remodeled or built a house before and was as ignorant as a coon hound would be. A friend asked me after the fact why I didn't consult her. I replied, "Because ignorance is ignorance. I didn't know I needed help!" True ignorance involves not knowing that you *are* ignorant.

I soon learned just how clueless I was when the music room walls turned out a beigy-salmon-pink color and the painter was mumbling something about how he'd never painted a kitchen pink either. I didn't know the paint I picked out for the kitchen was pink. It didn't look pink on the swatch, for crying out loud. I thought those little paint cards were to figure out what color I wanted. Nobody told me to buy paint samples and apply them to part of the wall to see what the color actually looked like on the surface before committing to it. So there we were with an ugly salmon-pink music room. I promise, the color on the swatch was blush beige!

Daniel, the soft-spoken dear, mildly informed me that he preferred moderate white for the music room. I said, "Oh, I don't know. I think we can work with this color. Once we get all the stuff in here and the decorations, it will be fine." The look in his eyes was one of near panic. Since the music room is his domain, I decided to go with his color choice. We had the painters redo the room.

After that shock, I took an emergency trip to the paint store and bought numerous samples to choose the colors for the rest of the house. Daniel calmly suggested we paint the entire house moderate white. I said, "But that's boring!" He said, "It's safe!" After the salmon-pink disaster and the threat of a pink kitchen, the poor guy was scared to death of what I might choose next.

Finally I found great colors we both liked. The whole house isn't moderate white, but the trim is. Daniel's happy. So am I.

I have no idea what brand the plumbing is or the details of the electrical wiring…and I don't care. The lights and water both work. That's all I need to know. I suggested we add a large laundry room off the family room, replete with a clothes chute from upstairs to down. Daniel thought that idea was fantastic, and it has been.

From what I understand, many couples nearly go to fist city over building or remodeling a house. We didn't have one angry moment. We did have one disagreement about another issue. Looking back, I think we were both so tired and stressed that the tense interchange was inevitable…and probably more healthy than if we'd suppressed our thoughts. According to Jack and Judith Balswick, "Conflict is to be expected when two distinct and unique individuals express themselves equally. Marriage without conflict often signifies that one partner has given up personhood; there is agreement, but only at the partner's expense."[1]

Overall our remodeling process was smooth and far from the verbal Armageddon some fall into. Why? Because neither of us is interested in pushing our own agendas forward. We care more about what the other thinks than whether or not we get our own way. And that characterizes our marriage.

The Submission Paradox

As with the word "leadership," the word "submission" often is assigned a meaning Christ never taught. It becomes an unhealthy tool for one person to use to dominate the other. Whatever spin is placed on submission, its interpretation should not violate Christ's command of "in everything, do to others what you would have them do to you" (Matthew 7:12). Whatever husbands expect from wives regarding submission, it should be something they also expect to be applied to them.

Wives who are taught one-sided submission do not usually celebrate or contribute wholeheartedly to the sexuality of marriage. However, I have known of some who used sex for manipulation. Aside from this, some wives believe their primary role is to submit. Often this is interpreted to mean, "Shut down. Do nothing. Go with the flow." And *that* translates into a dull and boring bedroom life.

Submit to one another out of reverence for Christ.

EPHESIANS 5:21

Sadly, the husbands who enforce one-sided submission don't truly cherish their wives because viewing them as a subordinate means the husbands value their wives less than they value themselves. Paul himself encourages men to "love their wives as their own bodies" (Ephesians 5:28). Cherishing involves placing a high value on the cherished one. No husband who places a high value on his wife will place her in a position he would not want to be in himself. When this happens, both spouses are left lonely and longing for an earth-moving relationship.

Surprisingly I've come to realize that I submit to my husband more than many wives submit to theirs, including some who strongly insist that submission is for wives only. The difference is that my husband returns the honor. Neither one of us is pushing for our own agenda in anything or using the Bible to demand that we always have the last say. Neither of us has to fall into the coping mechanism of manipulation. We're free to be completely honest. When we're faced with a decision, if we both don't agree, we just don't do it. We wait and pray about it until God makes His perfect will clear to both of us. Donald and Robbie Joy have this to say about who makes the final decisions:

1. The person to whom responsibility and authority has been assigned by prior consensus.

2. By marital consensus, if the decision is regarded as too complex or far-reaching for either spouse to act alone.

3. If there is no consensus, postpone until there is consensus. Make no decision until both spouses own it.

When people respect each other, they will not demand a quick decision or take things into their own hands to satisfy their appetite for instant gratification. Instead of serving as a sort of "veto power," when mutual respect and mutual submission are in place, reluctance is recognized by the other spouse as a legitimate reason to wait...Manipulation through use of shame or guilt can dissolve the trust in a "two become one" mystery marriage. So mutual respect and mutual submission always mean: "If you cannot get the consent of your mind or heart right now, we need to wait, even let this opportunity pass." In a marriage, that attitude carries a deeper meaning: "You are more important to me than having what I want right now."[2]

This type of marriage takes spiritual maturity. Too many times marriage concepts focus on who has the most territory or authority, much like the disciples who focused on who was the greatest or who got what spot in the kingdom. When both spouses dare to fully submit and surrender their wills to the Lord, territory and submission issues cease because all the territory belongs to Christ. As mentioned in chapter 2, we are *mutual* stewards of God's territory, as He originally intended in the beginning.

The one who is on the throne of our home and marriage is Jesus Christ. Not Daniel. Not me. Jesus. I'm not trying to manipulate my husband into doing what I want. He's not using Scripture to insist he gets the final say. Both of us are fulfilling Paul's command to "submit to one another out of reverence for Christ" (Ephesians 5:21).

Healthy submission is unconditional love in action. As with love, saying submission is a role is like saying salvation is a role. Jesus Christ was the supreme example of submission. As Christians we are called to model Christ in every relationship we have, including our marriages. This leads to unity, peace, and healthy submission for both spouses.

When couples embrace the tie that binds, fighting for control stops. When the couple comes to a matter where they disagree, instead of arguing or insisting upon their own way or manipulating one another, they pray together until they come to a compromise or discover what God really wants. Wives stop viewing their husbands as a father figure and are free to view their husbands as their lovers. Husbands stop viewing their wives as childlike dependents and are free to love and respect their wives as adults. Both spouses are focused on serving and empowering each other, giving all they have to each other.

A blazing love affair ignites between the couple as they truly become one and grow closer and closer to each other. Sexual and emotional frustrations end for both spouses. The couple grows into a marriage that transcends time and culture...a marriage like God intended when He created Adam and Eve in the garden of Eden.

The Equality Paradox

Jesus never told people to *focus* on whether or not they were equals either. And if we aren't careful, equality itself can become a territory issue. If people fight over their equal share, equality is lost. Instead of fighting for all the territory, they're fighting for their equal share of the territory. But the goal is the same: *"Mine! Mine! Mine!"*

When both spouses surrender their wills to Christ and to each other, an amazing equality is indeed the by-product. But it's an equality that's bred at the foot of the cross when *both* spouses stand side-by-side as one and allow Christ to be Lord. They embrace His words as their motto and never foist concepts upon the other that violate His teachings. Neither spouse is demanding equality, but both are focusing on serving and making sure the other has equality

> *For this reason a man shall leave his father and his mother, and be joined to his wife; and they shall become one flesh.*
>
> GENESIS 2:24 NASB

in all things.

I believe the apostle Paul understood this well. He said much about equality and was highly concerned at some points that equality be carried out in marriage and in the church. In this passage Paul is referring to the church:

> Our desire is not that others might be relieved while you are hard pressed, but that there might be equality. At the present time your plenty will supply what they need, so that in turn their plenty will supply what you need. Then, there will be equality (2 Corinthians 8:13-14).

The next passage references marriage:

> Nevertheless, because of sexual immorality, let each man have his own wife, and let each woman have her own husband. Let the husband render to his wife the affection due her, and likewise also the wife to her husband. The wife does not have authority over her own body, but the husband does. And likewise the husband does not have authority over his own body, but the wife does (1 Corinthians 7: 2-4 NKJV).

This next verse can apply to marriage and the church:

> There is neither Jew nor Greek, slave nor free, male nor female, for you are all one in Christ Jesus (Galatians 3:28).

These are but a few examples. However, the best and most honest and practical scholarship methods occur when we not only define Paul by Jesus but also define Paul by Paul. Not only should we not interpret Paul in a way that contradicts Jesus, we also shouldn't interpret him in a way that has him contradicting himself. "All Scripture is God-breathed and is useful for teaching, rebuking, correcting and training in righteousness" (2 Timothy 3:16).

Scripture must be interpreted within the context of its surrounding verses as well as the greater framework of the Word of God. Don and Robbie Joy refer to this as "interpreting within the 'big picture' and reconciling within the ultimate context of what is biblical."[3] Joseph Coleson states, "The foundational principle of biblical exegesis is that 'Scripture interprets Scripture.'"[4] Ultimately methods of biblical interpretation must be developed that bring agreement among *all* texts.

The Hierarchical Paradox

Marriage is our last, best chance to grow up.

JOSEPH BARTH

As already mentioned, there are a variety of takes on marriage in the Christian church. The one that has been taught the longest is the Hierarchical Marriage Model. When evaluated historically, the hierarchical marriage was once viewed as a strict dictatorship, with the husband as ruler. It has gradually evolved in the United States into a moderate hierarchy with the husband slightly elevated in the marriage and home, and both spouses are said to be of "equal value," which is double-talk. In some ways this is a blending of yesterday's views that men are one rung higher on the value scale than women and today's strong cultural thrust toward equality.

I have numerous friends who are firm about having a hierarchical marriage. Many of these folks are good, God-fearing people who are devoted to their churches, are great citizens, and are a delight to be around. I don't believe these couples are purposefully living out domination, manipulation, codependency, passive-aggressive behavior, or any other negative coping mechanisms. However, many subconsciously fall into mild forms of these behaviors without realizing it.

From the wife's perspective, one "manipulation" is taught through the generations. What many husbands don't know or only vaguely know is that some wives in traditional hierarchical marriages are really the ones running the show. There's this pact passed down from mothers to daughters, from older female friends to younger: "Honey, you just make him *think* he rules, but outwit him at every turn." One of my friends put it this way, "You always get your way, you just make him *think* he's getting his way." This aside was acknowledged *after* she vehemently stated that men rule. And when a wife is silently manipulating her husband to get her own way, she's not equally valuing him any more than the husband who views his wife as a subordinate.

Many times people who support the hierarchical view of marriage stress that the husband and wife are equally valuable, but the wife ends up submitting more, especially when a final decision must be made—and that power is the husband's. If the wife and husband really are equally valuable, why don't they share an equal say? This is like telling a slave he's equally valuable to his master, but the slave still "gets" to be owned. If he's really equally valuable, then why isn't he equally free? When equal value is truly practiced, spouses share an equal level of autonomy and God-approved power.

Often an analogy is drawn between marriage and corporations, saying that one person has to be in charge so that decisions can be made and work continues smoothly. The problem is that Scripture never says we are to model our marriage after business models. There's no other relationship on the planet like marriage. It's a unique, intimate union...a mystery, as Paul says in Ephesians 5:32. If there's any institution that should model mutual respect and the freedom found in Christ it should be Christian marriages.

In *Two Become One: God's Blueprint for Couples,* Donald and Robbie Joy state,

> In any organization or ongoing set of relationships, certain responsibilities "go with the territory." Where authority has been fixed by consensus (that is, by mutual respect agreement), it is clear that the responsibilities to make decisions belong to that person. In the most complex organizations, even a heathen one, a chief executive officer could not possibly make all of the decisions alone. It is inconceivable that any committee of two (e.g., a marriage) would elect officers.[5]

Unfortunately, many marriages aren't based on equal autonomy and power or true mutual respect. They're often based on one-upmanship and manipulation, which flies in the face of Christ's teachings. The husband likely uses the Word of God to prove he has the final say, and the wife in turn may be silently manipulating him and laughing up her sleeve. Ironically, I've heard men and women in these marriages crowing the loudest and longest about wives submitting to their husbands.

Many manipulative coping mechanisms fall under the label of Passive-Aggressive Personality Cluster. In a website monitored by Steve Mensing, M.Ed., a counselor and life coach, passive-aggressive is defined as:

> a learned behavior often developed in response to over-controlling parents during childhood. Later this "over-control" might be projected onto authority figures like bosses, teachers, and spouses. Sometimes this unassertive behavior may be modeled within families. Because it's learned behavior, passive-aggression can be replaced by developing an awareness of this behavior and the anger behind it as well as learning and applying assertive behaviors.[6]

A few of the characteristics of the passive-aggressive personality are:

- "Attacking" others through passive means. Thus the aggressive intent is cloaked by the passive method.

- Hiding disagreement or hostility while being nice to someone.

- Agreeing to do something they oppose and then not following through, doing the opposite, or secretly doing what they wanted to do anyway.

- Voicing an opinion they don't really hold in order to keep the peace and then silently manipulating the scene to go their own way.

- Saying things they don't believe because that's what people want to hear.

- Saying one thing but acting out what is true to their inner feelings—often through manipulation and control.

- Being afraid of letting honest feelings show because they desperately want to please people.

- Feeling compelled to believe things or act in a way they're opposed to.

- Giving in to others to avoid conflict because they believe they must avoid conflict at all cost because they'll never win.

- Being afraid to show anger so they act out anger through silent manipulation.

- Squashing and denying their own feelings rather than upsetting another person by disagreeing with them.[7]

Just as the codependent woman hides behind the Hierarchical Model of marriage to support her codependency, so the passive-aggressive woman hides as well. Many times passive-aggressive behavior goes hand-in-hand with codependency.

I recall an episode of the TV sitcom *Happy Days,* set in the 1950s, that perfectly illustrates this point. Joanie Cunningham wanted a new dress. Her mother, Marion, suspected that Mr. Cunningham wouldn't agree to spending money on new clothes. So she instructed her daughter on how to get the dress she wanted. They went shopping and brought home two outfits on approval, which means they'd make their decision and take one back the next day.

Marion told her daughter exactly what to do. Following her mother's advice, Joanie put on the first outfit—a skimpy short set—and sashayed into the living room. She paraded in front of her father, asking him if she could buy it.

> *For everyone who exalts him-self will be humbled, and he who humbles himself will be exalted.*
>
> LUKE 18:14

He went into orbit, saying in effect, "No daughter of mine is going to dress like that!"

The women "bowed" to his authority and went into the other room so Joanie could change into the dress she really wanted. As Marion predicted, her husband was very pleased with this second, more modest outfit. He said, "Oh, yes. I like this one. It's very pretty, and you're nice and all covered up like you should be." He agreed to buy the dress. When the women left the room, he looked at the camera and admitted, "I think I've just been manipulated." Of course this was all for fun and entertainment… but the truth is that's often how many marriages are. And the issues at stake are much, much bigger than the purchase of a dress. There's nothing honest or humble about a husband and wife relating to each other this way. The emphasis is on power and control, rather than honesty and freedom. Neither side honors God or fulfills the teachings of Jesus Christ. Instead, there's one dysfunctional coping mechanism layered on top of another.

Prayer Points

* Examine your heart before God and ask Him to show you what your goals are in your marriage.

* Once you realize your goals, ask the Lord to help you eliminate any unhealthy goals and strengthen the healthy ones.

* Pray that the Lord will bring you and your mate to healthy submission: unconditional love in action.

- Ask the Lord to show you where you and your mate have failed each other. Pray for the courage to discuss with your mate the wounds that have been inflicted because of those failures.

- Ask God to give you the strength to honestly confess and break free of any passive-aggressive behavior.

Love and Romance

Ask your spouse to make a list of six romantic things he or she would enjoy and that you could do. Tell your spouse that the things on the list need to be lots of fun and something you can reasonably accomplish or set up. Spend the next several months fulfilling that list.

> "In a love-based marriage, both spouses focus on empowering each other, not manipulating to get their own way."

The Sex Question

Marriage should be honored by all,
and the marriage bed kept pure.

HEBREWS 13:4

Dear Diary,

For my fiftieth birthday this year, my wife (the dear) purchased a week of personal training at the local health club for me. Although I am still in great shape since playing on my college football team 30 years ago, I decided it would be a good idea to go ahead and give it a try.

I called the club and made my reservation with a personal trainer named Belinda, who identified herself as a 26-year-old aerobics instructor and model for athletic clothing and swimwear. My wife seemed pleased with my enthusiasm to get started! The club encouraged me to keep a diary to chart my progress.

Monday: Started my day at 6:00 AM. Tough to get out of bed, but it was well worth it when I arrived at the health club to find Belinda waiting for me. She was something of a Greek goddess—with blonde hair, dancing eyes, and a dazzling white smile. Woo hoo!

Belinda gave me a tour and showed me the machines. She took my pulse after 5 minutes on the treadmill. She was alarmed that my pulse was so fast, but I attributed it to standing next to her in her Lycra aerobics outfit. I enjoyed watching the skillful way in which she conducted her aerobics class after my workout today. Very inspiring.

Belinda was encouraging as I did my sit-ups, although my gut was already aching from holding it in the whole time she was around. This is going to be a *fantastic* week!

Tuesday: I drank a whole pot of coffee, but I finally made it out the door. Belinda made me lie on my back and push a heavy iron bar into the air, and then she put weights on it! My legs were a little wobbly on the treadmill, but I made the full mile. Belinda's rewarding smile made it all worthwhile. I feel *great!* It's a whole new life for me.

Wednesday: The *only* way I can brush my teeth is by laying the toothbrush on the counter and moving my mouth back and forth over it. I believe I have a hernia in both pectorals. Driving was OK as long as I didn't try to steer or stop. I parked on top of a Geo in the club parking lot.

Belinda was impatient with me, insisting that my screams bothered other club members. Her voice is a little too perky for early in the morning, and when she scolds, she gets this nasally whine that is *very* annoying.

My chest hurt when I got on the treadmill, so Belinda put me on the stair-monster. Why would anyone invent a machine to simulate an activity rendered obsolete by elevators? Belinda told me it would help me get in shape and enjoy life. She said some other odd things too.

Thursday: Belinda was waiting for me with her vampire-like teeth exposed as her thin, cruel lips were pulled back in a full snarl. I couldn't help being a half an hour late; it took me that long to tie my shoes.

Belinda took me to work out with dumbbells. When she was not looking, I ran and hid in the men's room. She sent Lars to find me, and then, as punishment, put me on the rowing machine...which I sank.

Friday: I hate that witch Belinda more than any human being has ever hated any other human being in the history of the world. Stupid, skinny, anemic little cheerleader. If there were a part of my body I could move without unbearable pain, I would beat her senseless with it, which wouldn't take long.

Belinda wanted me to work on my triceps. I don't have any triceps. And if you don't want dents in the floor, don't hand me the stupid barbells or anything that weighs more than a sandwich.

The treadmill flung me off, and I landed on a health and nutrition teacher. Why couldn't it have been someone softer, like the drama coach or the choir director?

Saturday: Belinda left a message on my answering machine in her grating, shrilly voice wondering why I didn't show up today. Just hearing her made me want to smash the machine with my day-planner. However, I lacked the strength to even use the TV remote and ended up catching 11 straight hours of the Weather Channel.

Sunday: I'm having the church van pick me up for services today so I can go and thank God that this week is over. I will also pray that next year my wife, the poor misguided soul, will choose a gift for me that is fun, like a root canal or a vasectomy.[1]

My brother-in-law sent this "diary" to my husband via e-mail. When my husband let me read it, I doubled over and laughed so hard I thought I was going to pass out. Hitting middle age has really changed my perspective on a lot of things, including my body. Unfortunately it doesn't look like Belinda's anymore. Anytime I hear a man 45 or older mention how good looking a 20-something woman is, I think, *Yeah, and after a week or two with her, you'd be in ICU on a respirator!* Belindas have a way of taking gumption out of older men.

My goal as a wife is to keep my husband so satisfied that a Belinda doesn't hold strong appeal. Granted, I know Daniel is a normal male and he'll notice a beautiful young woman. He'd be dead if he didn't. However, there's a big difference in noticing the obvious and lingering over "what ifs."

The truth is, our sexuality is a big part of who we are as human beings. How often do you hear sermons about this geared toward married couples? Besides the "do not commit adultery" part, seldom does the church as a whole teach on this subject. I suspect this is mainly due to embarrassment or not knowing how to address this personal issue. Granted, talking about sexuality in a Sunday morning service isn't all that appropriate considering the wide variety of members and visitors, and any pastor who did so would probably be out of a job.

When I wrote *Romancing Your Husband,* I had no idea what God was opening up for me. I just knew He'd laid the book on my heart after my marriage was revolutionized. I never dreamed people from all over would e-mail me, asking me about married sexuality or pull me aside at conferences and ask me questions about sex. But after a few years of writing about marriage and holding marriage seminars, I've come to realize that God has called me to talk about this subject and encourage couples to celebrate the sexual aspect of their relationship. In today's climate of blatant sexuality, I'm amazed at the number of people who are very uncomfortable listening to someone address the topic, even in an appropriate setting with adults only.

At the beginning of my reaching out to help women, I said, "I am not Dr. Ruth. I'll be glad to answer anybody's questions, but I'm not a sex expert." Still, people kept coming to me with their questions. The ones I knew the answer to, I'd answer. The ones I didn't know the answers to, I'd find them. This has now been going on for years. After the last conference I looked at my two girlfriends who were co-speakers and commented, "Maybe I *am* a Dr. Ruth sort, and I've just been in denial. People keep asking me questions about married sexuality, and I keep answering them." My friends laughed out loud.

I know God has called me to this. One thing that helps is that I've never been embarrassed about sexuality. I think I was born without an embarrassment gene. My husband usually says "Amen!" to that. (He *was* born with an embarrassment gene, by the way.) Even though I was sexually molested when I was young, I've worked through the baggage and come out on the other side with a healthy attitude and a desire to encourage couples to experience a vibrant bedroom life. Although I've never formally been schooled in sexuality, I have a dynamic marriage and I've done quite a bit of study.

Part of my vision for Tie That Binds ministry is to show couples how to break out of restrictions, embarrassment, and hang-ups, and then educate them on the freedom they have through Christ in *every* aspect of their lives— including sexuality. As I share some of the questions I've encountered when

I teach and interact with people via e-mail, I hope you'll be inspired to take a fresh, liberating view of God-given sexuality. I do believe setting and audience need to be considered when talking about bedroom intimacies and discussing sexual technique, but I also believe there's far more to sex than the physical aspect. Even if a couple has perfect technique, relationship issues in the marriage will inhibit their sex life. Furthermore, if either of the spouses has sexual baggage their sex life is not going to sizzle.

In their book *Red-Hot Monogamy*, Bill and Pam Farrel discuss the differences in attitudes on sex. The Farrels point out that children of the 60s and 70s are far more open about discussing sex while "others prefer to keep the lights off and their mouths shut when it comes to the area of sexuality. The children of these couples may wonder how they ever got here because Mom and Dad never talk about sex."[3] Well, we're going to dare to discuss sex today.

> *Scores of young men and women. . .were fed a lot of false and harmful ideas by well-meaning but ignorant parents and preachers. Now they are unfit for marriage, unable to be husbands and wives who can live without fear, guilt, and shame. Damaged? Yes, badly damaged.*[2]
>
> DAVID A. SEAMANDS

How do I recognize sexual baggage?

In the ideal world, all parents would have Daniel's and my attitude toward sexuality. They'd view sex as a normal, healthy part of life because God created sex. They'd prepare their kids for marital fulfillment. In the ideal world, both spouses would be virgins on their wedding night and neither would ever stray. Neither spouse would have sexual hang-ups or negative baggage. They'd enjoy a great sex life from the start to the end of their marriage. When God's perfect plan is carried out from the beginning of a marriage, sex is usually good...very good indeed.

But that isn't the way most marriages happen. According to David Seamands, "In our society, it is very difficult for anyone to grow to young

adulthood without suffering some damage in the sex department of his
[or her] personality."[4] Many times one or both partners have had negative sexual experiences, including rape, molestation, and forced fondling.
Other times, one or both may have committed sexual sins. And even if
both spouses are virgins one or the other might be eaten up with sexual
shame or guilt because of parental silence or shame-based views of sexuality.

Often the people who don't want the topic of sexuality covered at a conference are the ones who have negative issues and are terrified of hearing the
subject discussed. As I've traveled the nation and ministered in churches
and at conferences, I've had men and women confess secret affairs, pornography use, homosexual liaisons, and participation in orgies. I've heard
reports of ministers losing their credentials due to pornography and affairs,
people in the church who leave their mates, sexual addictions of all sorts,
and on and on.

Since so few people honestly discuss sexual issues these days, when church
people encounter someone who does talk about healthy, God-ordained
sexuality, they feel they can safely and freely confide. And do they ever!
I've gone into regions and had people tell me things they would never tell
their pastors...and haven't told anybody else either for fear of condemna-
tion and consequences. I'm a "safe" person to tell because names and faces
blur into a sea of thousands. And chances are I'll never meet the people
again. The bottom line is that churches are full of people with sexual baggage and issues—from the pastor who has a stack of porn in his closet to
the wife who is frigid and unable to break free because her mother taught
her sex was dirty or evil.

For couples to have a great sex life, they have to be willing to deal with their
sexual baggage, which includes any negative or sinful sexual experiences
a person has been involved in that create guilt, shame, emotional pain,
mental discomfort, and/or thwarts or inhibits a vibrant sex life. Working
through the baggage involves getting honest with God and each other and,
if necessary, seeking a trusted counselor. It also requires patience. The
healing process takes time.

God's will is not for you to live with your sexual self in bondage. The Lord is not ashamed of sex. He created it. Take your sexual issues to Him. Ask Him to remove the chains that keep you locked up and give you directions for what you can do about them.

How do I recognize sexual addiction?

Of all the sexual baggage people have, addictions are some of the most prevalent and the toughest to work through. Most of the time sexual addictions for men involve obsessive masturbation with pornography and casual sex (sometimes with prostitutes). Sexual addictions are usually acted out in private, so many people manage to hide their problems for years. Eventually it overtakes their lives though.

Women also develop sexual addictions. They can get sucked into pornographic movies and magazines and become obsessed with masturbation. Although women tend to fall prey to "soft porn," the addiction is still as real as hard porn. I recently received an e-mail confession from a woman who developed an addiction to sexually explicit romance novels. The problem so overtook her she was spending all day reading while neglecting her home and family. These books are readily available at most stores and are as dangerously addictive as X-rated magazines. Just as many teenage boys begin sexual addictions in junior high, so do many teenage girls under the guise of reading a "little romance novel." And just as teenage boys often get exposed to pornography by stumbling into their fathers' stash, so teenage girls can become addicted by picking up their mothers' novels. (And girls can pick up negative messages from their fathers' magazines, just as boys might from their mothers' books.) Most secular romance novels these days are far from biblical in their content—even the tamest ones.

(There are quite a few romance novels that are decent, and several publishers offer Christian-based stories. I write Christian romance novels, and I've had wives tell me their marriages were healed when they read about the devastation of divorce or when a character showed how to cope with loneliness. Jesus Christ taught in parables, so clean storytelling is a great way to minister to people. There are some decent romances in the secular market. But women and girls need to be careful and guard against bathing their minds in sexually explicit novels.)

> For any substance or behavior to be addictive it must involve the chemistry of the brain. Feelings of sexual pleasure and excitement involve this brain chemistry. Powerful neurochemical reactions are involved in very basic parts of the brain that create intense feelings of pleasure. If God had not built us this way, we would not procreate. It is a natural part of God's design...As with many addictions, sexual feelings can be used to escape painful emotions. If the sexual activity is new, exciting, or dangerous, the adrenaline it brings can elevate an addict's mood. If the feelings are about romance, touching, being held, and the orgasmic experience of sex, powerful opiates in the brain can have a relaxing effect. If depressed, an addict can elevate his or her mood. If anxious or stressed, the person can depress his or her mood.[5]

Sex addicts seek to modify the same problems as those who use mood-altering drugs to escape. Either way, the addiction is as strong as if the person were hooked on alcohol or heroin...and just as hard to break. Like other addicts, sex addicts don't purposefully set out to do sleazy things or be bad people. Many times the problems that contributed to the addiction started in their families of origin, and this addiction is part of a family network of dysfunction. Addicts are usually hurting individuals who found something that made them feel okay for a while. Unfortunately it's a trap they eventually can't get out of on their own. Another aspect is highlighted in *The Pornography Trap:* "Dr. Patrick Carnes says sex addicts are shame-based individuals who don't believe that anyone really knows or likes them or that anyone could possibly meet their needs. Sex becomes their most important need...Sex addicts are also very dependent, though they may act powerful."[6]

Mike Courtney is very open about his fall into sexual addiction. He was a successful pastor who could grow a church like crazy. But he had a major problem. Now in recovery, he has a life coach ministry in which he helps other Christians overcome addictions. He encourages couples to work through compulsion issues together and keep their marriages intact.

Fortunately, he and his wife are a living testimony to God's miraculous power to renew and rebuild what Satan tried to destroy.[7]

Everyone isn't as fortunate. For a sex addict to recover, he or she has to take responsibility for his or her own behavior and *seriously* seek help. When an addict agrees to receive help, the spouse should be involved in the recovery. When dealing with addictions, more often than not the spouse is codependent and enables the addict, sometimes subconsciously, to continue the destructive behavior. Silence, denial, and covering or making excuses for un-acceptable behavior don't encourage healthy behavior. Often when addiction manifests itself in a marriage, *both* spouses come from families where addictive tendencies of some sort were lived out. In that situation, *both* spouses need to work through their issues.

Mature people accept and confess their mistakes and shortcomings. Immature people seek to deny problems, minimize mistakes, and blame others.[8]

How do I overcome rape or molestation?

As bad as sexual addiction is, the ugliest stories I've heard are of men and women who have been sexually brutalized through rape or molestation. The atrocities they've suffered have horrifically scarred them. These types of stories make me furious! What some people do to others is scary.

After my talk at one event, a woman came to my book table. She was shaking and gently weeping. She asked, "How do I find help? When I was a child my father repeatedly molested me. He'd get together with his drinking buddies, and he'd molest me...and then give me to his friends to molest me." This was a way of life for her as a child. Now in her late fifties, she still couldn't have a healthy relationship with her husband. I gave her some books in hopes she'd find a grain of healing, and I strongly encouraged her to pray and seek long-term counseling.

As someone who was molested, I understand a portion of this woman's pain. But it still blows my mind that a father would repeatedly assault his own daughter and then hand her over to his friends to do so as well. And I've heard similar stories from other women, so I know this isn't an isolated problem.

The ugliness of sexual molestation and rape requires therapy. And it's not something a man or woman usually recovers from overnight. Satan's primary weapon against victims is silence. He knows that if he can injure us sexually we are often covered in so much shame we just can't talk about it. And that's like covering a wound full of gangrene with dirty rags. The infection gets worse and eventually destroys.

If you've experienced the ugliness of sexual abuse, allow the Lord to walk you through the painful memories. Find someone to talk with. Sometimes well-meaning church people lose patience with those who are sexual victims and tell them to "just get over it." Or they're amazed that a sexual victim is still hurting over something that happened 20 or 40 years ago. These good-hearted, well-meaning people don't understand the dynamics of deep, emotional woundedness. They often believe if you have enough faith, you should recover immediately. And God can do that, but in my experience He usually opts to help people work through their issues over time. When you encounter someone who doesn't understand, stop sharing. Find someone who can and will listen, be attentive, and help you through your healing. Many times that someone is a licensed, trained counselor. God works through these people who act as His loving, comforting arms and hands. Healing is worth the financial and time investment.

Healing from sexual violation takes time, and recovery can't happen unless you're ready to get honest. Jesus is the ultimate source of knowledge and wisdom for our marriages. He's also the healing balm regarding sexual healing. He cares about every element of our makeup—including our sexuality. He asked an invalid, "Do you want to get well?" (John 5:6). That might seem like an odd question, but the truth is some people *don't* want to get well. They want to hang on to their past—the injuries and pain—because they believe the woundedness gives them a license to be weak and not grow.

Achieving wholeness is work. It involves releasing resentment, refusing to embrace the abuse as part of your identity, and, eventually, forgiving the abuser. (That doesn't mean that if legal remedies are available you shouldn't file charges. The abuser needs to be stopped.) Depending on the extent of the sexual injury, this journey can take a few months or several years. Often God brings healing in layers, like an onion being peeled. Just as wounds to the body take time to heal, so sexual wounds take time to heal. Once they're uncovered and exposed through prayer and honesty, God begins His miraculous process. More extensive physical wounds take longer to heal; likewise more extensive sexual wounds take longer to heal. A person who was fondled by an elder sibling a few times will heal faster than one who was repeatedly gang raped by relatives, "friends," or strangers.

As important as honesty and counseling are, there's no replacement for sitting in the presence of God and allowing Him to pour His healing Spirit into your soul. In my journey toward healing, I've taken the anguish and anger and fear to the foot of the cross and been still before the Father. I let the power of listening to soft, worshipful music and God's presence penetrate my heart like sweet honey from heaven…sometimes for an hour at a time, several times a week. During that hour, I fell silent and allowed God to bring to my mind the things He wanted to show me. During my healing process, He walked me through the pain and healed one memory at a time. This practice is a must for wholeness and healing.

Please don't give up hope! I am living proof that God can and does perform miracles. Without the power of God, no woman who's been molested would be able to write a book titled *Romancing Your Husband* and teach and encourage other women to become their husbands' lovers. God did that for me. And He will help you heal too.

Why is my sex drive stronger than my husband's?

The following e-mail is a compilation of many I've received through the years.

I'm writing to tell you that I just finished reading your book *Romancing Your Husband,* and I am frustrated. You see, I'm the one in our marriage with the higher sex drive. My husband shows little or no interest in sex. If I try to initiate sex, he thinks I'm pushing him. I want sex several times a week, and he only wants sex once a month. I feel like I'm going to explode. Is there any help for women like me? Am I alone?

It's not always the man who has the hot sex drive! In an ideal situation, the husband and wife will be equal in their sex drives, but we don't live in a perfect world. According to David Clarke, "About twenty-five percent of husbands fall into this category [of low sex drive]. If you're doing all you can to be sexy and show interest, and he's not responding, then he's the one with the sexual problem. It could be anything, including unresolved past pain, resentments against you, too much stress, age, fatigue, and lack of confidence in his ability to perform."[10] In her book *Is That All He Thinks About?* Marla Taviano supports Clarke's observation with the following list:

Having sex in marriage that is both enjoyable and fulfilling depends on so much more than the biological mechanics of sex. We believe that God intended it that way.[9]

- He's too tired.
- He's afraid he won't be able to perform.
- He has guilt left over from premarital sex.
- He's afraid of getting his wife pregnant.
- He's not attracted to his wife.
- Work takes up all his time.
- He has control issues.
- He's bothered by his wife's sexual past.
- He fears emotional rejections.
- There are problems in the marriage.
- He's involved with pornography.
- He's having an affair.[11]

Some men just don't have high sex drives. That doesn't mean they're having affairs or read pornography. And there's not necessarily anything wrong with them. They just aren't wired that way. But sometimes it's more than that. I know of one man who was convinced he was impotent. He couldn't respond to his wife. She eventually had an affair and divorced him. During the process, he realized his wife had some very serious problems that manifested themselves in their marriage relationship. When he remarried an emotionally healthy woman, he quickly discovered he wasn't impotent at all!

The best thing to do is find out the reason for the low libido. Check to see if there are medical causes, current studies show that many men in America have low testosterone. If there are sexual issues, deal with them. Seek counseling if necessary. Get really honest. Find out if there's something either one of you are doing that creates a wall in your marriage. Many times men are erroneously painted as emotionless beings who can have sex anytime. That's not totally true. Male sexuality can be affected by relationship issues.

> *Let him kiss me with the kisses of his mouth—for your love is more delightful than wine. Pleasing is the fragrance of your perfumes; your name is like perfume poured out. No wonder the maidens love you! Take me away with you—let us hurry!*
>
> SONG OF SONGS 1:1-4

If none of these issues apply to your marriage, are you (or your mate) willing to consult a physician or a pharmacist for recommendations on vitamins designed to increase libido? These vitamins are available for both men and women. They do work. Some organic food stores or health food stores also carry such supplements.

When a husband and wife have worked through their sexual baggage and approach married sexuality with freedom and as a celebration of their union, God smiles. He created sex and the ways male and female bodies respond. I am convinced the Lord wants spouses to have a blast with each other. As part of your marriage revitalization create your own private sexual revolution that will have you both rushing home for more!

What do I do if my mate wants to bring someone else into our bedroom?

The woman who posed this question shared that she'd gone along with him verbally because she was taught she is to submit to whatever her husband wants. She said they haven't brought another woman in yet, but she really didn't feel right about the whole idea.

This question came to me privately after a small group meeting of "nice little church ladies." There are many things women (and men!) in the church are facing or have done that they would never dream of telling their peers.

Having sex with someone besides your marriage partner is prohibited throughout Scripture. Exodus 20:14 states, "You shall not commit adultery." Even if both spouses agree to having what contemporary culture calls a "ménage a trois" or "threesome," it's still adultery. Just because both spouses consent to including another man or woman in their bedroom or to switch spouses with another couple doesn't mean it isn't against God's principles.

My husband, Daniel, met a man who was very distraught because his wife submitted to his coercion to swap spouses for one evening. They'd joined another couple and traded mates. Part of the deal was to all have sex in the same room together. The toll on the wife's emotional and spiritual health was significant, and their marriage suffered. Some couples "court" other couples in attempts to get them to eventually agree to swap partners for sex. Don't fall into this trap. The devastation this type of activity brings into marriages includes guilt and shame that eventually torments and may destroy the people involved.

A "threesome" or having "extra" partners is really a small orgy, which Scripture specifically calls sin:

The acts of the sinful nature are obvious: sexual immorality, impurity and debauchery; idolatry and witchcraft; hatred, discord, jealousy, fits of rage, selfish ambition, dissensions, factions and envy; drunkenness, orgies, and the like. I warn you, as I did before, that those who live like this will not inherit the kingdom of God (Galatians 5:19-21).

Contemporary pornography makes "threesomes," orgies, and swapping partners look exciting and inviting. But the Bible doesn't state that such sexual practices are sin because God is a starchy being who just isn't "with it." No, it's because the results are damaging and deadly to marriages, including a fragmentation of the union, a lessening of mutual commitment to each other, emotional scarring, exposure to diseases (VD, HIV), and other problems.

Another aspect of this question is the problem of submission. Scripture tells wives and husbands to submit to each other: "Submit to one another out of reverence for Christ" (Ephesians 5:21). However, the Bible also states,

Avoid every kind of evil. May God himself, the God of peace, sanctify you through and through. May your whole spirit, soul and body be kept blameless at the coming of our Lord Jesus Christ. The one who calls you is faithful and he will do it (1 Thessalonians 5:22-24).

Furthermore, 1 Thessalonians 4 parallels the sanctification process with sexual purity:

It is God's will that you should be sanctified: that you should avoid sexual immorality; that each of you should learn to control his own body in a way that is holy and honorable, not in passionate lust like the heathen, who do not know God; and that in this matter no one should wrong his brother or take advantage of him. The Lord will punish men for all such sins, as we have already told you and warned you. For God did not call us to be impure, but to live a holy life. Therefore, he who rejects this instruction does not reject man but God, who gives you his Holy Spirit (verses 4-8).

Balanced teaching on marriage relationships looks at the broad scope of *all* Scripture and comes to conclusions that are theologically sound. Yes,

Scripture does tell husbands and wives to submit to one another, but that admonishment must not be interpreted in a way that requires either spouse to disobey biblical morals.

For instance, God's Word tells us to obey the laws of the land. But the Old Testament story of Shadrach, Meshach, and Abednego is a good example of righteously refusing to submit to the law because it would involve idolatry (Daniel 3). These Jewish men refused to bow to and worship the king as god, even though that was the law of the land and they were commanded to. They did not submit to the authorities because that would violate their allegiance to God and His laws. Therefore they were cast into a hot furnace. God came to their rescue and honored their faith. In the New Testament, when Peter and other apostles were pressed to choose between obeying man or God, they said, "We must obey God rather than men!" (Acts 5:29). Likewise, God has not called wives or husbands to submit to the other to the point of sin.

And when it comes to sin, the Lord holds both wives and husbands accountable for their actions. Women who submit to their husbands in every instance, including sinful practices, are putting them in the place of God in their lives. And husbands who engage in sinful practices suggested by their wives are choosing their mates over God. Both of these instances involve idolatry, just as it did for Shadrach, Meshach, and Abednego when they were commanded to bow to the king.

What if my mate wants to do something sexual I'm uncomfortable with?

The first concern is whether your mate is asking you to do something sinful or just out of your comfort zone. The Bible is clear about the activities that are wrong: bestiality (Leviticus 18:23), homosexuality (Leviticus 18:22; Romans 1:26-27), adultery (Exodus 20:14), and sodomy (Genesis 19:1-11). Anything such as pornography, orgies, watching others have sex, or bringing other partners into the union is classified under adultery. And activities that are violent, painful, demeaning, and involve coercion clearly go against biblical injunctions to love, respect, and honor others. Aside from these practices, everything else is okay, barring having sex in public, which could get you thrown into jail anyway.

I've received scores of e-mails through the years from people who are worried that some of the most elemental sexual practices are sinful, including having sex in more than one position. So many people have sexual baggage! From being taught as children that sex, even between married partners, is dirty to being exposed to pornography early, people in our culture often struggle with sexuality. Some believe that anything other than a quickie in the missionary position is sinful. I was recently told of a husband who had so much sexual baggage that he and his wife only had sex once in two decades of marriage—and that was to conceive a child. He was terrified of his sexuality because of what he'd been taught as a child.

God *wants* Christian couples to celebrate and enjoy each other in the bedroom. After all, He created us as sexual beings, and He made sex a delightfully pleasurable experience. If your partner wants to try something new and it isn't sinful, be open and willing to work through sexual inhibitions. Discuss your reservations with him or her. Express your apprehension and ask for time to warm up to the idea. Think about taking small steps toward the suggested activity. In the process, come up with something new *you'd* like to explore. Then try your mate's idea and yours in the same week.

If you absolutely can't come to terms with what your mate suggested, keep brainstorming together. You might dream up something even more exhilarating!

Speaking openly, there is a thing or two on my "can't do" list that aren't sinful. Thankfully, Daniel and I have great communication so this isn't an issue for us. Our hesitations have nothing to do with sexual baggage or fear. Instead it's personal preference, like some people prefer chocolate and some prefer vanilla. Everybody is different. Find out what pleases your mate and be willing to express any new ideas you have as well. Respect your mate's comfort zone if he or she just can't get into a new idea. You'll find that as you grow and explore together your "can't do" list may get shorter and shorter. In the healthiest marriages both partners are willing to celebrate their sexual relationship by being spontaneous, creative, and fun!

For more information on sexual expression check out my books *Romancing Your Wife* (specifically chapter 4, "Great Sex 101") and *Romancing Your Husband* (specifically chapter 5, "Communication and Sex"). For creative products, romantic games, and books to enhance married sexuality, you can check out the "Romancing Your Marriage" section at www. debrawhitesmith.com).

What's the healthiest way to teach my kids about sex?

In Daniel's and my parenting, our goal is to model the kind of parent God is and incorporate the teachings of Christ into all aspects of relationships. God set forth His law and told His followers to either obey Him or live with the consequences of their choices. So we tell our kids, "Here are the rules...and here are the consequences. If you choose to break a rule, you have to live with the consequences." Then we make sure we don't rescue them from the consequences. For instance, say our teenage son, Brett, begs me to buy him a new shirt. So I do. Then we get home, he wears it once, and decides he hates it. What are the consequences of getting me to pay for something he casually discards or refuses to use? What are the consequences of wasting money? Brett becomes financially responsible for the item. He pays for it. And that tends to change everything. Now when he asks for something and decides capriciously he doesn't care for it, he voluntarily continues to wear or use it!

What if your kids are younger? When our daughter, Brooke, was younger, she wanted to wear a hot shirt in 100-degree weather. She was adamant about wearing it even though I told her she'd sweat like a sow. So what did I do? I let her wear it. And, yes, she sweated a lot. No, I didn't bring another shirt for her to change into once she realized I was right. I didn't rescue her. I let her live with the consequences of refusing to listen to wise advice. (I did make sure she had plenty of water and monitored her so she wouldn't get heat stroke.)

Teaching your kids about choices and consequences and letting them make choices and feel the effects of any consequences of their own choices early on when issues are small helps them catch on that rules are generally for their benefit. Now that Brett and Brooke are teens, they understand more that Daniel and I are reasonable, fair, and honest. (If you are unreasonable, constantly angry and critical, you'll break your children's spirits, which hurts them and your relationship with them.) Since our children learned at an early age how we operate and that we follow through, they trust us when we say, "Here are God's laws on sex. There are bad consequences if you break them. And you'll regret your decision for many years." They're listening and they get it because we've followed God's example.

Daniel and I also look at the patterns Jesus exhibited when He was with His disciples. He was their "spiritual parent." He told them the truth about everything and *prepared* them for the future—for His crucifixion, His ascension into heaven, and His being physically gone but spiritually present with them. We attempt to do the same thing with our children. It is our assignment as parents to *prepare* our kids for adulthood because we won't always be around to guide them. And part of the preparation definitely involves talking with them about sex.

I have talked to my kids frequently about sex since they were preteens. My daughter and I had "the talk" in my van just before she turned 9. It was an impromptu discussion that happened because she asked a couple of questions I couldn't answer without being forthright about the particulars. I answer all their questions as they come up and pragmatically model an attitude of sex as a God-created part of life. And it is!

I have regularly told my son, now 17, how his thought processes will change as he goes through his teen years and what to expect, what is normal and healthy for a teen boy to feel. I also share what behaviors are good and what cross over the decency line. I continually tell him there's nothing to be ashamed of when his brain starts focusing on sex because that's the way God made him. I also emphasize that he needs to learn how to manage and save this God-given gift of sexuality for marriage. When opportunities present themselves, I explain how to know if a girl is coming on to him and how to avoid being seduced—necessary knowledge for young men these days. I also warn him about the pitfalls of pornography, acquaint him with the traps, and let him know he can come to Daniel and me if he ever has questions, needs help, or falls prey to a problem so we can help him. Nothing is too embarrassing to share or talk about.

That's the kind of parent God is. If we do get seriously tangled in sin, we take our trouble to Him, and He comes alongside us until we break free. He *never* enables us to continue in that sin, and He doesn't rescue us from the consequences. But He helps us get free and learn from what we've done.

I don't want either of my children to have a layer of shame over their sexual selves when they get married. Part of parenting responsibility is to teach them about sexuality and equip them for successful marriages. Since sexuality is a big part of marriage, Daniel and I are committed to age-appropriate discussions that give them the information they need. My husband and I have decided that before our kids get married, he will tell our son the necessary details of how to have an exciting sex life and I will provide similar information to our daughter.

Having one pre-puberty talk with our kids doesn't fulfill our parental duty. We don't want to send our kids out into the world without knowing about sexuality and how to handle it appropriately. We're also committed to guarding and even fighting for their purity. I want my son and daughter to understand the dynamics of a potentially tempting or hazardous situation. I also want to equip them so they won't fall prey to temptation. I remind my son periodically that boys his age are sometimes into porn, and I've provided specifics about how to resist if someone tries to share smut. I tell my daughter what older boys say when trying to take advantage of girls. Even when my kids were younger, I never let boys and girls play together behind closed doors. I monitor them closely. I have told my kids that children can molest and experiment on other children, and that can be just as damaging as an adult's advances. I've done this in a safe, private environment using wording and materials that are appropriate to their ages and honor healthy sexuality.

Unfortunately, some people equate purity with ignorance. They believe that the less sex is talked about and the more rigid the rules, the more pure children remain. But that doesn't hold true or ensure purity. Quite the contrary, sometimes ignorance and parental rigidity is a precursor to wrong sexual choices. A child who is uneducated in a healthy and biblical manner will not know how to deal with bad situations. In *The Pornography Trap*, Ralph Earle and Mark Laaser state if a person "grew up in a rigid family with very little understanding of God's grace, he or she will be more likely to break the rules."[12] An "innocent" child may not understand what's happening when he or she is approached inappropriately until it's too late. And then he or she may not know what to do.

I repeatedly tell my kids that sex is a wonderful gift from God. It's like the best Christmas present in the world. But the time to unwrap and celebrate it is when they are married. Then it's time to party! This gives them a balanced view and teaches them sex is not bad or shameful; it's something terrific meant for marriage relationships.

Prayer Points

* Ask the Lord to reveal anything in your life that might become a sexual addiction.

* If past sexual addictions or infidelity shadow your marriage, pray for the courage to talk through the issues until God has completed the healing.

* Ask God to show you if or how you may have contributed to the addiction or infidelity of your mate.

* Pray for God's healing for any sexual woundedness. Be willing to bask in His presence long-term until that healing can be completed.

* If your mate doesn't share your libido, pray that the Lord will give you wisdom in discussing the issue and that He will work in helping you and your mate come to a solution.

- Pray that God will erase any embarrassment that's stopping you from discussing sex with your kids in a balanced and healthy manner.

Love and Romance

Set aside a special time with your mate for a sexy brainstorm session. Make sure you allow plenty of time. Find a location and time that's best for both of you, maybe a candlelit dinner, a stroll on the beach, a picnic, or a cozy time in front of the fireplace. Tell your mate what the topic is ahead of time so you both can be thinking of ideas. Then talk about your new ideas for the bedroom. Ask God to anoint your time together and give you both new insights to celebrating your sexuality. After you've brainstormed a while, you might be so enthused you'll want to immediately put some of your new ideas into practice. Go for it!

"In a love-based marriage, sex is celebrated
and both partners are generous lovers."

Free to Be

The body is a unit, though it is made up of many parts;
and though all its parts are many, they form one body.
So it is with Christ. For we were all baptized by
one Spirit into one body—whether Jews or Greeks, slave
or free—and we were all given the one Spirit to drink.

I CORINTHIANS 12:12-13

Freedom in Christ

One of the great things about centering your marriage on Christ, rather than cultural tradition, is that both spouses are free to be who they are. Neither is tied to a cookie-cutter mold from any time era and told he or she must

All the world's a stage, and all the men and women merely players. They have their exits and their entrances, and one man in his time plays many parts.

WILLIAM SHAKESPEARE

fill that image. There is not a one-size-fits-all set of roles that might rub in all the wrong places. Each person is as different as shells on the beach; God created each of us with unique gifts, talents, and insights. To unleash these gifts, talents, and insights into the marriage, each spouse has to be aware of which ones he or she holds.

I think we sometimes confuse values with traditions and create a gospel that ties people to a mold God didn't create. Some couples get so focused on being what everybody else says they're supposed to be that they lose sight of who they really are. The individuality that God created in them dissolves as they attempt to adapt to what tradition defines as their goals.

In *Ordinary People, ExtraOrdinary Marriages,* Brian Nystrom states,

> Prior to the fall Adam and Eve did not know about their nakedness
> (Genesis 3:10-11). In their state of innocence, they were free to be who
> they were. They were not trying to make themselves look good on the
> outside, because they didn't have to be afraid of showing who they really
> were. They had committed no sin, so they showed how it was. We, how-
> ever, have sinned, so we do not want to show how it is. Instead we show
> what we think others want to see, in order to gain their acceptance. This
> is shame-based behavior.[1]

In chapter 1 we observed:

- God is free to be God.
- Jesus is free to be Lord.
- The Holy Spirit is free to flow through marriages and homes to
  heal and deliver and empower.

When Jesus is the tie that binds, not only do both spouses give free access
to their hearts and homes to the holy trinity, they also give freedom to
each other. Each spouse is free to be who he or she is and free to celebrate
that individuality.

For years I read countless marriage books that detailed what a husband
was supposed to be like. Often these books described men as focused,
goal-oriented, driven, natural leaders (per Webster's definition) who have
an urge to explore and discover the world at large. Because of this I grew
more and more disillusioned with my husband because he is the total
opposite of this. He's laid back, quiet, and happy to just be. He enjoys traveling but isn't interested in going out to conquer for the sake of conquering.

And in the same books women were said to be more laid back and happy
to just be nesters. But I'm not, and I figured that meant I was odd. In my
marriage I am the one who is focused, goal-oriented, and wanting to rattle
and explore the greater world. So I became discouraged.

Finally I realized I was expecting my husband to be everything I was, and I was expecting me to be everything he was. From there, I analyzed the scene and discovered that many well-meaning people confuse gender differences with personality differences. Men are often assigned my "mover-shaker/explore the world" personality type, while women are often assigned my husband's "laid back/chill out at home" personality. These misconceptions come through cultural stereotypes. And too often people try to fit in to them or are forced in to them when that's not who they really are.

Let's set aside the stereotypes and cultural expectations and explore what genuine gender traits you hold that make you different from your mate. We'll also take a look at some tools to help you evaluate what personality types you and your mate have. The bottom line is that all men are not Choleric "John Wayne" types and all women are not wilting vines. Robert Hicks writes:

> I have known creative men of unique abilities in the arts. These sensitive, sometimes compliant spirits struggle with the "role" of being leader in the home. Are they less a Christian because they find it difficult to express a John Wayne type of masculinity? Are they less men because of the personality and talents God gave them? When I read the simple statements of Scripture to them, they are set free. Rather than offering a role to play or a set of rules to follow, I let the simple imperative rest with them. I ask, "What does it mean for you to love your wife as Christ does the church?" I allow each individual to figure out what it means in terms of his personal marriage dynamics. Often, the applications men come up with are far more insightful and loving than anything I may conceive.[2]

Differences Between Men and Women

This great e-mail touches my funny bone while highlighting gender stereo-types:

How to Make a Woman Happy

It's not difficult to make a woman happy. A man only needs to be a friend, a companion, a lover, a brother, a father, a chef, an electrician, a carpenter, a plumber, a mechanic, a decorator, a stylist, a sexologist, a gynecologist, a psychologist, a pest exterminator, a psychiatrist, a healer, a good listener, an organizer, a good father, very clean, sympathetic, athletic, warm, attentive, gallant, intelligent, funny, creative, tender, strong, understanding, tolerant, prudent, ambitious, capable, courageous, determined, true, dependable, passionate, compassionate.

Without forgetting to give her compliments regularly, love shopping, be honest, be very rich, not stress her out, not look at other women.

And at the same time he must also give her lots of attention but expect little himself, give her lots of time—especially time for herself, give her lots of space, never worrying about where she goes.

While also never forgetting birthdays, anniversaries, and arrangements she makes.

How to Make a Man Happy

Show up naked. Bring food.[3]

In the previous chapter we discussed that some men have weak libidos—approximately 25 percent. That leaves approximately 75 percent who have strong libidos. According to Dr. David Clarke, when men list their top 9 priorities in life, it goes like this:

1. sex	6. sex
2. sex	7. sex
3. sex	8. sex
4. sex	9. food[4]
5. sex	

For many men, this list is fairly accurate. A main difference between most men and most women is the level of their sex drive. If this doesn't apply to you, that's what this chapter and book are all about. You're free to be the female with the higher sex drive or the male with the lower sex drive. Nobody is going to despise you or think less of you.

Dr. Clarke lists the following as the priority list for women:

1. children	6. health
2. family	7. job
3. friends	8. finances
4. home	9. sex[5]
5. church	

This list doesn't wholly fit me, and the first list doesn't wholly fit my husband. He's very much relationship-oriented and concerned about our family and children. When I asked him what his list would look like, it was nearly identical to mine. I rank husband, family, children, and home as competitors for number one. Under God, they each hold high importance in my heart. It's very hard for me to rank them. I didn't tell my husband this, and he said the exact thing to me. After these, Daniel ranked health because you can't have sex without good health. Then sex was next. I believe a big part of the reason Daniel and I have such a phenomenal home life is because our priorities aren't based on self-interest and are in the right place.

With that said, I believe Dr. Clarke's lists do point to the fact that, in general, many men are more sexually focused while many women are more relationship focused. After all, stereotypes are usually formed for a reason. However, I've gotten enough e-mails from men who bewail the fact their wives aren't relationship focused that I know there are others who don't fit the traditional pattern.

Dr. Gary Smalley says women are the relationship monitors in the marriage. Most women are born with a relationship manual that supplies them with instinctive knowledge of how a great relationship should function.[6] I believe most men are born with a sexual manual and have instinctual knowledge of what a blow-your-socks-off sex life will be like. I believe the reason God created the genders with these two distinct "manuals" is because it takes *both* to have a dynamic marriage. When both husband and wife are free to contribute their gifts and insights to the marriage, it becomes a stronger, dynamic union.

Sex drive and relationship insights aren't the only difference between men and women. There are several other basics, such as the way we think and process information. For the most part, men tend to be compartmental thinkers while women's thought processes flow together like a river. This is a biological issue, not a cultural issue.

Compartmental thinking is set up when the male hormone hits the brain of a fetus. The hormone severs some of the ties between the left and right brain, limiting left brain/right brain communication, which results in less fluidity in thought processes.

Only when the male hormone enters the fetus does it undergo the changes that are distinctively masculine. The same testosterone that makes all the masculine physical changes to a fetus is also responsible for affecting the way men think. Bill and Pam Farrel's book *Red-Hot Monogamy* is all about this issue. According to the Farrels,

> Men process life in boxes. If you look down at a waffle, you see a collection of boxes separated by walls. The boxes are all separate from each other and make convenient holding places. That is typical of how a man processes life. A man's thinking is divided up into boxes that have room for one issue and one issue only…[In contrast]…women process life more like a plate of spaghetti. If you look at a plate of spaghetti, you notice that individual noodles all touch one another. If you attempted to follow one noodle around the plate, you would intersect a lot of other noodles and you might even switch to another noodle seamlessly. That is how women face life. Every thought and issue is connected to every other thought and issue in some way.[8]

Because of these waffle boxes, men's minds are often less connected to the overall scene than women's are. Oh, they're connected to whatever compartment they're in, but men may be clueless to what's going on elsewhere. Women can be in one room of the house and hear a child fall out of a swing in the backyard and immediately know there's a problem. Men often don't hear a thing unless they're in the backyard or near a window because they're totally focused on whatever they're working on.

Once both spouses understand this about each other, it's important to respect and appreciate the opposite gender's thought processes. I avoid "verbally crashing" my husband's compartments when he's focused on something. I give him time to change focus before I go into detail about something. Otherwise I might get snapped at—not because he's being mean but because I burst into his compartment and disrupted him. Likewise, Daniel respects my spaghetti thinking process and appreciates my ability to multitask like crazy. There are times when I need the strength of his "waffle" thinking, and there are times he needs the strength of my "spaghetti" thinking. We come together to complete each other, as God intended.

As founder of a national ministry and a businesswoman, I've purposefully developed some compartmentalizing skills. I had to in order to stay sane. When I have so much going on—raising kids, running a household, and numerous book projects contracted—I've learned to file things away in my brain and not allow myself to think about them. Otherwise, I'd be overwhelmed. And this is true for most women. Women can learn to compartmentalize, and I've encountered men who have developed the ability to multitask. They have busy lives, several things going at once, and they handle it. Once again, this is a skill most men have purposefully developed. I don't know how a single father could manage small children any other way. While both skills can be developed, it's good to understand that most men are born with a natural ability to compartmentalize, and most women are born with the natural ability to multitask.

Aside from sexual or relationship focus and the differences in our thought processes, men are usually more physical in their communication, while women are more verbal. When my son wants to let his male friends know he likes them, he'll give them a good shove. The friends shove right back and are content to know, "That guy's my friend." When my daughter wants to let a friend know she likes her, she talks to her...on the phone, via e-mail, and text messaging. The more girlfriends talk, the more they feel loved.

Personality type also affects gender traits. Quieter women naturally talk less. Women with stronger personalities are more likely to have a stronger sex drive. Furthermore, some men are less physically aggressive than others. For instance, my husband is the strong, silent type. Despite his athletic build, he's never engaged in physical fighting. It made no sense to him. During his school years, when someone tried to start a physical altercation, he walked away. He didn't want to hurt anyone. However, he did love football and other contact sports and turned into a goal-oriented gorilla during football games. My son, who is a husky child, can't stand the thought of contact sports. Nevertheless, he still relates to his dad through physical contact such as playful punches and shoving. Aside from this, he is a talking machine who loves drama and singing because his personality type is like mine. However, my daughter still talks circles around him.

> *Personality is to a man what perfume is to a flower.*
>
> CHARLES M. SCHWAB

Discovering Your Personality Type

First understand that personality types are asexual. These character traits have no gender. People's personalities are formed through the natural temperament they are born with as well as by the environment they are raised in. Because of this, I have male friends and associates whom I am "just like," and female friends and associates whom I am the opposite of. True, male associates with like personalities to mine might tend to think compartmentally and be more sexually focused in their marriages and more physical in communication, but our basic natures are the same. The men who share my Choleric/Sanguine personality type are goal-oriented, fast-thinking, movers and shakers who grab their problems by the horns and throw them to the floor. You'll never find these guys roaming the mall "just looking," and you won't find me there either unless it's on behalf of a mother–daughter time with Brooke. (She loves to roam the mall.) For men and women with our personality type, we have our list, buy what we need, and go on to the next thing on our agenda. We have business to take care of, and we take care of it.

Our female friends and associates who share my husband's Phlegmatic/ Melancholic personality type are laid back, gentle souls who, in my husband's immortal words, "enjoy being in their rut." These women can roam the mall for hours and be content to just watch people. The males meander around in the tool section at Sears and purr like kittens the whole time, absorbing the ambience of all those wonderful gadgets. Porch swings and hammocks were made for them. They're often a calm source of wisdom.

Fortunately most people marry their opposite personality type. I used to get so exasperated over Daniel's rut because my goal in life was to obliterate ruts. I'm as strongly Sanguine as I am Choleric, and Sanguines are like rubber balls that bounce all over the place. But now that I'm more mature, I realize that Daniel's "rutness," as he calls it, has kept me out of trouble many times. He's forever catching my leg as I sail upward. He says, "You might want to think about that. Look at the pitfalls." I've learned through the years to listen to his wisdom and make adjustments. I'm sure he's stopped me from being decapitated a time or two or twenty.

On the other hand, I keep him from getting too comfortable in that ditch of his. I'm forever bumping him out for a spell and encouraging him to loosen up a bit. He's learned spontaneity can be fun, especially when he's the "victim" of one of my romantic schemes. I've helped him develop a sharp and snazzy wardrobe. Left to his own devices, he'd wear black, brown, and army green and be quietly happy in his nondescript clothing.

We balance each other. And once we fully understood our basic personality types, it made us better appreciate each other. Our knowledge also helped us understand one another and know what to expect from the other. For instance, if our house was on fire, I'd run screaming through the place, gathering up everything I could salvage and corralling the kids to get out into the front yard. Did I mention I'd be screaming the whole time? My hair would be on end as well. Daniel, on the other hand, would probably calmly stroll toward the front door and, without ever raising his voice, say, "The house is on fire. Might be good for us to mosey on outside now."

Now, let's take a closer look at the four basic personality types: Choleric,

Sanguine, Melancholic, and Phlegmatic. Most people manifest strong traits of two personality types, with one more dominant than the other. Many will also have a few characteristics of a third personality type. For instance, I'm Choleric/Sanguine with an analytical Melancholic streak. Daniel is Melancholic/Phlegmatic with a fun-loving Sanguine streak.

As you read the following descriptions, you will probably be able to make a pretty good guess as to what personality type you are. However, I highly recommend you visit www.thepersonalities.com and discover all the wonderful resources Florence and Marita Littauer offer for those wanting to discover more about their personality and their mate's. You can also take a personality test right online or order one by mail. I owe my education on the personalities to the Littauers and their great collection of published material.

Also, a fun analogy I always use when I speak is that of the *Winnie the Pooh* characters. These characters were created with a real awareness of the four basic temperaments. After reading this chapter, rent a *Winnie the Pooh* video and observe the behavior of the characters I mention. Even though *Winnie the Pooh* is a child-targeted series, it is an excellent tool for observing personality types. You'll be surprised at how you can clearly see the four temperaments at work...how they rub each other the wrong way and complement each other. You'll also begin to recognize yourself and others in them.

Choleric

Cholerics are movers and shakers who get things done. They are decisive, bold, tenacious, and inspire respect by their sheer willpower. In the corporate world, Cholerics often get to the top. They are optimistic, outgoing, and are usually the upfront people who have plans and the goals to go with them. They have the weakness of being abrupt at times and can come across as insensitive. If not careful, they can sacrifice feelings for the goal.

This is the personality type that has been traditionally assigned to men, so these traits are often viewed as masculine. But many women have Choleric personality traits. According to Robert Hicks,

> It is hard for me to imagine the amount of harm that has been done to Christian husbands, wives, and children in the name of…destructive mythology. Over the years, I have counseled women who struggle with their outgoing, "unsubmissive" personalities. They reveal internal struggles of how it seems God cursed them with a kind of personality that just gets them into trouble. When I pastored in one of our eastern states, I met many professional women who were assertive and used to speaking their own minds.[9]

If you're a female with a Choleric personality, you've probably experienced the frustration of not fitting the traditional mold of what a "good, godly woman" is supposed to be. But there's hope! I've turned my strengths to things of God and allowed Him to use me to His glory. Even though my personality type is Choleric, that doesn't give me the license or right to barge ahead of my family or husband, nor should a man with this personality type do the same to his family or wife.

In the *Winnie the Pooh* lineup of characters, Rabbit best fits the Choleric personality. He can be testy and bossy and intolerant of those such as Tigger, who just wants to bounce around and have fun. But Rabbit is a focused dude who gets things done!

Sanguine

Sanguines are upbeat, outgoing types who love parties and jump into things with both feet—sometimes without thinking about consequences. They love people and are often popular. You can usually spot a female Sanguine by the size of her earrings—usually large hoops or shiny rhinestone numbers. Male Sanguines are usually dressed with flashy ties that contrast with their suits. As for jobs and hobbies, Sanguines are often cheerleaders and encouragers. Their conversations are full of expressions such as "How exciting!" and "How wonderful!" They're often public relations people who love the world. These people can be absentminded, too willing to change the agenda without considering the implications, and somewhat naive. They also have a tendency to be late. Their motto is, "I'm here! Who cares if I'm late? I made it, and that's the important thing!"

Many times the Choleric and Sanguine personality types are complementary and combined in an individual. What you get in that case is a bossy cheerleader.

In the *Winnie the Pooh* lineup, Tigger is Sanguine. That cat bounces around on his tail and doesn't have a clue about the havoc he's creating. In one book I used to read to my kids, Tigger drives Rabbit crazy because he's hopped through Rabbit's carrot patch and messed up all his goal-oriented work.

Phlegmatic

Phlegmatics are often introverted, quiet people. They are usually cooperative, laid back, and easygoing. A Phlegmatic man is considered dependable and called the "strong, silent type." If a woman is Phlegmatic, she's considered naturally sweet and submissive. Phlegmatics make up their minds slowly. They often sit rather than stand, and are probably responsible for inventing many shortcuts. My husband dreams up all sorts of inventions that make life easier. I think a Phlegmatic invented the hammock, can opener, and probably the modern washer and dryer and dishwasher.

These people enjoy working behind the scenes, but they're notorious for being motivated only when they're interested. You'll seldom catch them being motivated for the sake of motivation. If my husband isn't interested in "it," he doesn't care if it gets done or not. If he's interested in something, his eyes turn "neon orange" and he's all over it.

The common blend with Phlegmatics is Melancholics, although some blend with Sanguines.

As for *Winnie the Pooh*, the most Phlegmatic is Winnie the Pooh himself. That gentle soul is happy to hang out and eat his honey. No bouncing around for him, and you can forget him being testy or getting bent out of shape. Pooh is the kind of bear you want to have around to smooth out rough edges. Pooh types are often viewed as "the most Christlike" in Christian circles because of their gentle natures. (No personality type is really more "Christlike" than the others, of course.)

Melancholic

Melancholics are often cautious and analytical. They gravitate toward detail-oriented work. They also enjoy analyzing Scripture. They can be suspicious of new concepts and don't easily change their minds. They're serious creatures who size up every situation and can tell you in a few seconds what can go wrong. Usually they're sure something *will* go wrong. Melancholics love being on time...in fact they can be obsessive about it. My husband is Melancholic as well as Phlegmatic, and I tell him he'd be happy if we got to church the night before and camped out so we'd be on time Sunday morning. Melancholics are more introverted if they're also Phlegmatics. The Melancholic/Choleric personality type is also common. In such cases, they are extroverted. Choleric/Melancholics usually want things done right the first time! Melancholics are often theologians or accountants who drive people crazy by analyzing everything. Emotionally they tend to get depressed, especially if they're also Phlegmatics.

Eeyore is the *Winnie the Pooh* character that best exemplifies a purely melancholic creature. The poor donkey drags his tail around everywhere. His main theme in life is "Woe is me. It's all going downhill from here." The good thing about Eeyore is that he's trustworthy. Pooh can count on him. At a recent marriage event, I met a couple who was nearly purely Tigger and Eeyore. The wife was up on the roof doing the tango, and the husband was as calm as an earthworm in a coma. However, they fully understood the personality type differences and appreciated each other exactly the way they were.

Once we receive a clear view of the issues of temperaments and how they affect who we are and how we react, we are more free to totally accept each other and celebrate our differences. In many instances, people marry their "complements." Imagine what conflicts can happen when opposites marry. Not only do they have to deal with understanding the different ways each gender thinks, but also grapple with opposite personality types. Think about Tigger, who doesn't care if he/she is ever late, married to Eeyore, who wants to be early everywhere. Or what happens when low-goal Winnie the Pooh marries high-goal Rabbit? When God puts opposites together, it's best to value your mate's strengths and blend together the best of who you both are. Trying to change your spouse into someone more like you won't work!

All personality types can successfully work together in a husband–wife union to create a whole…just as both waffle and spaghetti thinking come together to provide balance. Marriage is like a puzzle. Each mate brings his or her pieces. As the years unfold, you keep adding your pieces to the picture. The pieces are shaped by gender differences, personality types, and God-given gifts. No man has every piece shaped the same, and neither does any woman. Nor is it God's will for every man or every woman to hold exactly the same set of pieces. I encourage you to explore and appreciate your mate's differences. Also get to know who you are. Understand you both need to be free to be who God made you to be. And then you can generously pour your gender and personality strengths into your marriage.

Florence and Marita Littauer also talk about those who have a "Personality Mask." These people project a personality in public that is not innately theirs. Often this happens to compensate for childhood issues or to please others. If you and your mate have been forced to wear such masks under the guise of "fulfilling roles ordained by God," the time has come to take them off. Christ said, "The thief comes only to steal and kill and destroy; I have come that they may have life, and have it to the full" (John 10:10). A full life can only happen by totally embracing Jesus and allowing Him to give you the freedom to completely embrace whom He created you to be.

Prayer Points

* Pray that God will give you the courage to step into the freedom of who you really are. The Lord accepts you as you are!

- Ask the Lord to help you appreciate and understand your mate's thought processes.

- Pray that God will give you the desire to meet your spouse's sexual needs, regardless of who has the higher drive.

- Ask God to give you the courage to embrace any relationship changes that need to occur for your marriage to thrive.

- Once you figure out you and your mate's personality types, ask God to empower you to help your mate and marriage with your strengths.

If you have anything really valuable to contribute to the world it will come through the expression of your own personality, that single spark. . .that sets you off and makes you different from every other living creature.

BRUCE BARTON

Love and Romance

First visit www.thepersonalities.com and order a couple of "Wired that Way" personality tests. Then set aside an evening for the two of you to experience a "Personality Date." Prepare popcorn and sodas or iced tea to set the mood for fun. Take the personality test, and then evaluate each other's strengths and weaknesses. Explore the issue of personality masking. If one or both of you are masking, dialog until you get to the root of why. If childhood issues are involved, this activity will possibly open the door to healing. Many times the same childhood issues that cause people to mask are the ones that drive dysfunctional behavior in other areas as well.

"In a love-based marriage, each spouse accepts the other
as he or she is and focuses on empowering,
rather than changing, each other."

Revolution Reflections

Introduction

I pray that by now your heart and mind have been opened to the voice of Christ in a new way. If your marriage was strong, I hope it's growing stronger; if it was weak, I hope it's improved; and if your marriage was about to end, I hope you've reconsidered.

The following Reflections will help you discover new truths on your own and empower you to connect on a deeper level with the Son of God and your spouse. Work through each reading alone or with your mate. If with your mate, be open to discussing any key issues that come up, even if sharing them brings embarrassment or shame. Don't be surprised how God can and will anoint His truth and your willingness to get gut-level honest with each other.

What Has Been Planted in Your Marriage?

A man reaps what he sows. The one who sows to please his sinful nature, from that nature will reap destruction; the one who sows to please the Spirit, from the Spirit will reap eternal life. Let us not become weary in doing good, for at the proper time we will reap a harvest if we do not give up. Therefore, as we have opportunity, let us do good to all people, especially to those who belong to the family of believers.

GALATIANS 6:7-10

Passage: Galatians 6:1-10

A parable I coauthored with Dr. Stan Toler, *The Richest Person in the World,* deals with reaping what we sow. This concept applies to finances, friendships, and family and marriage relationships. Throughout the New Testament there is reaping and sowing imagery. When we look at nature we also see the same principle at work. God created a miraculous system of seed germination in nature...and the same applies to us.

After I finished cowriting the novel, I reflected upon how we each have sown things throughout our lives, but we also have had things sown in us. Sowing has been done by our families of origin...parents and siblings. Some by friends and acquaintances. Some "crops" sown in us are good and some are bad. Just as bitter weeds grow in a garden, so "bitter weeds" planted by bitter deeds can grow in us. These weeds can take on the form of negative or sinful behavioral patterns, sour attitudes, bad habits, or inappropriate coping mechanisms to cover wounds from harsh treatment.

If we don't recognize these weeds in our lives and allow God to remove them, they can and will hinder our marriages. Such weeds include unhealthy attitudes toward sexuality, behavior that splinters unity, and disrespect.

But there can also be an absence of sowing good things in our lives. For instance, a person who has never been taught how to be romantic will not know how to do so in a marriage. Although it's important to recognize the weeds in our lives, we also need to acknowledge when something is lacking so we can plant seeds to compensate for or eradicate problems.

Whether we need to pull some bitter weeds or plant some good seeds, the answer to ending negative patterns and creating good ones lies in our willingness to be open with ourselves, with our memories, with God, and with our mates. This requires strength to acknowledge there is a problem and the willingness to allow God to show us clear memories of how the problem germinated in our lives. Then we must ask the Lord to forgive us for allowing the bitter weeds to flourish and show us how to plant healthy seeds that will help us be healthier.

Last, we need the confidence, security, fortitude, and transparency to talk the issues over with our mates. When very deep or tragic issues are involved, sometimes a trusted friend or counselor can help. But often the simple act of discussing the problem with our mates until we no longer feel pain or no longer manifest negative behavior is key to allowing God to retrain us.

When I yearned for more romance and excitement in my marriage, I began to assertively "plant the seeds" of exhilarating romance. The seeds took root immediately and showed an early growth that catapulted our marriage into something magnificent. But this wonderful state fully bloomed when Daniel and I were transparent with each other. This fostered deep emotional and romantic intimacy.

So many times we pray for miracles in our marriages when often the steps to our success are already laid out in the Word of God. Granted, there are some prayers that will only be answered by direct intervention of God.

But many times the miracle God wants to perform involves our recognizing we have things in our hearts that must be removed and then allowing Him to uproot them.

"Therefore confess your sins to each other and pray for each other so that you may be healed. The prayer of a righteous man is powerful and effective" (James 5:16).

> *Dear Father, please show me what has been planted in my marriage by me, my mate, or others that does not bring glory to You. Give me the fortitude to stop denying any bitter deeds that have spawned bitter weeds. Give me the courage to be transparent with You and my mate so we can pull up any weeds.*

Avoiding Poison

The Word became flesh and made his dwelling among us.
We have seen his glory, the glory of the One and Only,
who came from the Father, full of grace and truth.

JOHN 1:14

Passage: John 1:1-18

A brief parable...

A group of church friends wanted to get together on a regular basis to socialize and play games. As a result, four couples formed a dinner club and agreed to meet at a different couple's house each month.

The lady of the house was to prepare the meal. When Janet and Al's turn came, Janet wanted to outdo all the others and prepare a meal that was the best any of them had ever eaten. A few days before the big event, she got out her cookbook and decided to have mushroom-smothered steak. When she went to the store to buy some mushrooms, she found the price for a small can was more than she wanted to pay.

She told Al, "We aren't going to have mushrooms because they're too expensive."

He said, "Why don't you go down in the pasture and pick some of those mushrooms? There are plenty of them right in the creek bed."

"No, I've heard that wild mushrooms are poisonous."

Her husband responded, "I don't think these are. I see varmints eating them all the time, and it doesn't seem to affect them."

After thinking about this, Janet got into the pickup and headed to the pasture. She picked the wild mushrooms and took them home. She washed them and sliced them. When she was done, she went out on the back porch and got Ol' Spot's dog bowl and put in a double handful. She even added some bacon grease to make them tasty. Ol' Spot didn't slow down until he had eaten every bite.

All morning long Janet watched the dog. The wild mushrooms didn't seem to affect him, so she went ahead and put them on the steaks. Janet hired a lady from town to come out and help her serve. The waitress wore a white apron and a little cap. Everything was first class. The meal was a great success. After everyone finished, they all relaxed, socialized, and played dominoes.

The lady who had been hired to help came out from the kitchen and whispered in Janet's ear: "Mrs. Williams, Spot just died."

Janet went into hysterics. After she calmed down, she called the doctor and told him what had happened.

The doctor said, "It's bad, but we can take care of it. I'll call for help, and I'll get there as quickly as I can. We'll give everyone enemas and pump out their stomachs. Everything will be fine. Just keep them all there and keep them calm."

It wasn't long before the wail of sirens approached. The EMTs arrived with their medical packs, syringes, and stomach pumps.

The doctor arrived shortly thereafter. One by one, they took each person into the master bathroom, gave him or her an enema and pumped out his or her stomach. After the last one was finished, the doctor came out and said, "Everything will be fine now."

After the medical personnel left, the guests were all looking pretty wan sitting around the living room.

The hired lady came back out and said to Janet, "You know, that fellow that ran over Ol' Spot never even stopped!"[1]

Miscommunication is one of the leading causes of problems in relationships. However, no communication can become a poison that destroys any chance of a happy marriage. Unfortunately, many couples don't communicate about core issues that plague them for decades...until it's almost too late.

What topics are avoided? Things others have done to spouses or stuff spouses have done to each other. Often bad experiences in childhood taint marriages. Children who are abused grow up and continue the learned abusive patterns in their marriages. Not talking about or denying problems is the same as eating poisonous mushrooms. It contaminates the emotions, which sickens the marriage.

What issues manifest in your marriage? Have you talked about them? Can you identify their roots? Shame-driven or embarrassment-driven silence is Satan's tool to keep people in bondage. Honesty-driven confession is God's tool for leading people to freedom. Christ is full of grace and truth. As spouses, we can emulate Him by speaking truth and extending grace in the midst of pain.

Lord, I don't want any poison mushrooms in my marriage. Give me the courage to break the silence regarding anything I need to discuss with my mate. Help me see that silence isn't always golden. Sometimes it's fueled by fear. Give me the courage to share my issues. Thank You.

Tough Love

*Then we will no longer be infants, tossed back and forth
by the waves, and blown here and there by every wind
of teaching and by the cunning and craftiness of men in
their deceitful scheming. Instead, speaking the truth in
love, we will in all things grow up into him who is the
Head, that is, Christ. From him the whole body, joined
and held together by every supporting ligament, grows
and builds itself up in love, as each part does its work.*

EPHESIANS 4:14-16

Passage: Ephesians 4

Usually when we hear the word "love" we think of a soft emotion that
gives warm fuzzies. In reference to romance it usually encompasses sexual
feelings as well. Granted, sex isn't love, but when a husband and wife are
in love they express that in a variety of ways, including sexually.

While love *can* give us a soft glowing feeling, true love is the toughest,
the strongest, the most lasting of human passions. Pure love will stand the
test of time and withstand any circumstances that try to come against it.
As the apostle Paul stated in 1 Corinthians 13, "[Love] is not self seeking"
(verse 5). True love is all about focusing on the other person and what is
best for him or her.

Sometimes what is best for the other person is the tough side of love.
Many times people mistake speaking the truth in love with always being
soft-spoken. If we believe speaking the truth in love always means being
gentle, we're wrong! Christ spoke the truth in love. There were times
when He spoke softly and gently, as when He encountered the woman at

the well. But other times He was tough and unyielding, such as when He confronted the Pharisees about their hypocrisy. When dealing with dysfunctional issues, sometimes love must be tough. Giving in to or ignoring someone's dysfunctional behavior in the name of "keeping the peace" or "showing love" enables the problems to continue.

The book of Ecclesiastes states, "There is a time for everything" (3:1). When it comes to sin that has held us in bondage, there is a time for confronting it until we are free. When both husband and wife tackle issues together, deliverance can and does happen more swiftly than if just one spouse takes them on. Dealing with sin and dysfunction starts with complete honesty and ends with resolution to the problem. Remember, excellence in marriage happens through refinement. Refinement comes through honesty with God and with each other.

Dear Lord, give me the courage to embrace the many facets of love and be willing to be tough to break free from any dysfunction that has crippled my marriage.

Affairs of the Heart

My lover is mine and I am his.

SONG OF SONGS 2:16

Passage: Song of Songs 2

During the last few years I have communicated with a number of wives and husbands who are concerned about their mates' other relationships. The scenario goes like this:

> My mate is very good friends with someone of the opposite sex. He/she spends lots of time with this person either on the phone or in person. I even overhear him/her talking about me and our marriage. I have expressed concern over this friendship, but my spouse repeatedly tells me that they're nothing but friends and I'm just being jealous.

Sometimes the friendship existed before the couple got married, so the mate has had a platonic-but-close friendship with this special friend for years and has no intention of putting boundaries on it. Often the spouse who is expressing concern feels deeply betrayed and frustrated. And well he or she should.

Many times what is going on is an emotional affair. Emotional affairs happen when a platonic friendship turns into a crush or thoughts are entertained such as, "If I were single, this is the person I'd go after." Sometimes light flirting happens. When the spouse involved in the emotional affair gripes or puts down his or her spouse or discusses negatives about the marriage, verbal infidelity has occurred. Often verbal unfaithfulness coupled with an emotional affair leads to sexual infidelity.

Emotional affairs resemble a sexually chaste dating relationship. When coworkers have emotional affairs, they regularly do special things for each other, such as bake cookies or small repair jobs. They might walk to their cars together at the end of the day and spend breaks and lunchtime with each other. Many times when a man has an affair with his secretary, she starts out doing thoughtful, wifely things for him. This grows into a friendship, which blossoms into an emotional affair, which eventually becomes sexual.

In order to combat any chances of an emotional affair, some Christians run every time they see someone of the opposite sex. This is really only necessary if the person is spiritually, emotionally, or sexually weak. In such cases, the remedy lies in strengthening the marriage and his or her relationship with God to the point that fierce loyalty to the spouse and the Lord overrides temptation.

People have to work and interact with people of the opposite sex. In our ministry, my husband and I are surrounded by male and female acquaintances and associates. We're both very careful to not let any of these friendships grow into a relationship that might lead to an emotional affair. If we sense someone is too interested, Daniel and I report to each other with a "What do you think? Am I being paranoid or do you think this person might be trying to warm up to me?" Many times Daniel and I validate what the other is sensing. Then we quietly put boundaries on that person. I've found that sometimes Christians who are wholly dedicated to the Lord can go from one emotional affair to another without realizing or recognizing what's happening.

Occasionally baking cookies for business associates or walking to a vehicle together or having a business-related lunch doesn't automatically mean someone is having an emotional affair. These deeds can be a necessity or simply a polite consideration and nothing more. However, it's wise to be on guard so that habitual kindnesses don't grow into more...not only for you, but also for the other party.

As the outgoing, friendly sort who talks to everyone, I've learned the hard way that those who are emotionally needy can view the offer of friendship as something more personal and serious. Now that I'm a much older and wiser woman, I'm polite but careful to never give men a reason to think I'm available emotionally or otherwise. I also frequently mention God, my husband, and my family and keep conversations benign.

If you or your mate has experienced an emotional affair, perhaps the marriage isn't meeting the needs or fulfilling the one involved in the affair. I'm *not* saying that the emotional affair is the fault of the other spouse, but I am saying that often trouble in a marriage can drive inappropriate emotional attachments. In most cases problems in a marriage exist because both spouses contribute in some way. If an emotional affair turns into a sexual affair, and then a divorce and remarriage occur, the people involved will likely fall into a similar dysfunction again.

Examine your heart for any signs of an emotional affair. If your spouse is uncomfortable with a friendship you nurture, put some boundaries on that friendship. Don't enable a spouse's inappropriate jealousies that are bred by control and insecurity, but be sensitive. If you're spending time with and getting attached to a person of the opposite sex, your spouse will sense that and voice objections. Listen to your mate. Don't discount what he or she says.

> *Father, please show me any emotional affairs I might be blind to. Also, make me aware of anyone who is too close to me. Help me put kind-but-firm boundaries on that relationship. I want to be faithful to my mate sexually, verbally, and emotionally. And, Lord, please give my mate the same desires. Give us the wisdom and discernment to avoid unhealthy emotional attachments that violate our wedding vows. Bring us to a point in our marriage where we can joyfully say, "My lover is mine, and I am my lover's" and mean it.*

Do You Want to Get Well?

When Jesus saw him lying there and learned that he
had been in this condition for a long time,
he asked him, "Do you want to get well?"

JOHN 5:6

Passage: John 5:1-25

Anytime there is an issue in marriage that violates the wedding vows, the question that must be answered is, "Do you want to get well?" A violation of the wedding vows can happen through sexual or emotional affairs, verbal infidelity, soft- or hard-core pornography, substance abuse, and other addictions. Deliverance happens when the spouse who is exhibiting the negative behavior wants to be healed and the other spouse wants wholeness badly enough to stop enabling.

According to David Seamands,

> This is what Jesus asked the sick man who had lain ill for thirty-eight years. Do you really want to be healed, or do you just want to talk about your problem? Do you want to use your problem to get sympathy from others? Do you just want it for a crutch, so that you can walk with a limp?
>
> The lame man said to Jesus, "But, Lord, nobody puts me into the pool. I try, but they all get there ahead of me" (verse 7). He would not look deep within his heart to find out whether he really wanted to be healed.[2]

There are some people who are sick as a way of life. These people go from one physical ailment to another. All they talk about is their recent sickness or the latest medication. Some people genuinely have bad health, but some "healthy" folks thrive on "being sick." When faced with a remedy that might relieve some of their suffering, they usually refuse to try it, saying, "That will never help. Why even try?" These people don't *want* to be well. Being sick is a career for them, a lifestyle, an identity.

Sometimes addictions can become the identity of the person they hold in bondage. The addict claims that identity and is ruled by it. Whether workaholism, sex, or relationship addictions manifested by one emotional affair after another, the addiction often becomes an entity both spouses support. One spouse acts out the addiction while the other spouse enables the one addicted through silence, making excuses, rescuing, or refusing to draw hard boundaries.

Deliverance is available for everything from dysfunctional coping mechanisms to full-blown addictions. In some cases the remedy involves gut-level honesty with each other and with God. Sometimes the healing comes over time through the wise advice and support of a godly counselor, but even then Christ must be present to orchestrate the healing. For deep-seated addictions, many times help happens through recovery clinics.

Whatever the methods of deliverance, the redemption is complete through repentance. Many people confuse an apology with repentance. Verbal apologies mean nothing when the behavior has not stopped. Repentance happens when one or both spouses turn from the behavior and pledge not to return. Full repentance often involves a soul-level repulsion for the behavior that once ensnared.

The bottom-line question is, How much does one or both spouses want their marriage to be healed? Do they want healing badly enough to fully repent and allow God to change them from the inside out?

Lord, please deliver me of any tendency to wallow in my woundedness. Help me want to be healed. I want my marriage to be whole. Give me the guts to admit if I've been contributing to or enabling a destructive problem my mate has. On the other hand, Lord, please forgive me if I'm the one who has clung to destructive behavior that is tearing apart my marriage. Please heal my marriage and make my spouse and me truly one. Give us the grace to stay true to You through the healing process.

The Joy of Being Content

I have learned to be content whatever the circumstances.

PHILIPPIANS 4:11

Passage: Philippians 4:10-20

The following e-mail reveals an important trait that applies to women *and* men.

A store that sells new husbands opened in New York City. Among the instructions at the entrance is a description of how the store operates.

You may visit the store *only once!* There are six floors and the attributes of the men increase as the shopper ascends the flights. There is a catch: You may choose any man from a particular floor or you may choose to go up a floor, but you cannot go back down except to exit the building.

A woman goes to the Husband Store. On the first floor the sign on the door reads: Floor 1: These men have jobs. She decides to keep going.

The second floor sign reads: Floor 2: These men have jobs and love kids. "That's great," she thought. "But I wonder what's on the next floor." She takes the elevator up.

The third floor sign reads: Floor 3: These men have jobs, love kids, and are extremely good looking.

Wow! she thinks, but she feels compelled to keep going.

She goes to the fourth floor and the sign reads: Floor 4: These men have jobs, love kids, are drop-dead gorgeous, and help with housework.

"Oh, mercy me!" she exclaims. "I can hardly stand it." Still she moves on to the fifth floor.

The sign reads: Floor 5: These men have jobs, love kids, are drop-dead gorgeous, help with the housework, and have a strong romantic streak.

She is so tempted to stay, but she continues to the sixth floor. The sign reads: Floor 6: You are visitor 31,456,012. There are no men on this floor. This floor exists solely as proof that women are impossible to please. Thank you for shopping at the Husband Store.

Meanwhile, across the street, a New Wives store has recently opened.

The first floor has wives who love sex.

The second floor has wives who love sex and have money.

The third through sixth floors have never been visited.[3]

Contentment with our mates can be a sticky subject. Many people simply aren't content with their mates and lie awake at night wishing there really was such a thing as a husband or wife store so they could trade in their current model for a new one. But as I'm sure you know, no one is perfect. Some of the flaws people manifest are the downsides of their personality type's strengths. For instance, a Sanguine loves to talk and can talk on the spot about anything. He or she makes a dynamic motivational speaker. But he or she may also struggle to know when to turn off the talk. Once you discover you and your mate's personality types, it's important to understand and respect his or her strengths but also accept his or her weaknesses as the quirks that make your spouse unique. All men aren't going to be great at everything. Neither are all women. While my husband is a phenomenal father, he's as disorganized as can be. And while my brain holds a stash of neat files that contains books and ideas and long to-do lists, I'm an unrepentant closet slob. At this point neither of us is taking any measures to improve these problems. One of the things Daniel has said to me over and over is that he believes part of the strength of our marriage involves our willingness to accept each other the way we are, flaws and all. Instead of criticizing the foibles, we make light of them and unconditionally love. Our motto is, "Live and let live."

If your mate's weaknesses don't involve moral issues, betrayal, addiction, abuse, neglect, or any other sin, it's best to major on the strengths and give grace for the weaknesses.

Lord, I don't want to be one of those people who are never pleased. Give me Your grace to unconditionally accept my mate, flaws and all. Help me to stop expecting my spouse to be Superman or Wonder Woman. Instead, give me Your eyes to see the quality of the person he or she really is and Your heart to love unconditionally. Also help me realize that my spouse is dealing with and giving grace for my weaknesses too.

Losing the Chains that Bind

Therefore shall a man leave his father and his mother,
and shall cleave to his wife: and they shall be one flesh.

GENESIS 2:24 KJV

Passage: Genesis 2:20-25

There can be no cleaving without leaving. A husband and wife cannot fully join to each other until they have severed dependence on their families of origin. While connection with extensive family networks can be a great source of support and encouragement, they were never meant to be a controlling factor in the lives of a married couple.

Many spouses are still as connected or even more connected to their families of origin as they are to their spouses. Clear signs of this are when one or both spouses excessively serve the family of origin and allow the family of origin to crash into their lives whenever and however they choose. There are no boundaries on the family of origin's impact.

Whether geographically close or not, extended family relationships can be unhealthy to a marriage. This enmeshment may show up as an adult child calling her mom several times a day and depending on her for support instead of her spouse. This often means the wife or husband is in second place to the mother. I've also encountered situations where sons place their parents before their wives, perhaps insisting that the wife conform to his parents' demands.

According to Dr. David Hawkins,

> Families, fellow church members, coworkers, friends, and acquaintances of all types are capable of damaging individuality. Families can

be too distant and detached from one another, but they can also be too close. It may be hard to picture too much closeness, but closeness can be stifling. When individuals are too bent on pleasing one another, healthy engagement gives way to unhealthy *enmeshment*.

- Each person has to know what the others are doing.
- No privacy and no appropriate secrets are permitted.
- Gossip is rampant.
- People tell one another how to behave and feel.
- People talk for one another.
- People tell others how the others are feeling or what they are thinking.
- One or more family members is overly controlling.
- The family has a "right" way to do things and no other way is tolerated.[4]

Before I heard the term "enmeshed families," I had developed my own definition for these behavioral traits: a big wad of tangled snakes writhing together and biting each other. My analogy was based on the realization that such families are tangled in each other's lives to the point that you can't tell where one starts and the other stops. And they often live from one "biting" episode to another. Or somebody is not talking to somebody else at any given time. It's a cycle of twisted, negative behavior.

When extended family units are enmeshed, often individual families are also enmeshed because that's the way the adults learned to relate. For instance, enmeshment happens in the parent–child relationship when a child is expected to fulfill the family's choice of career. Enmeshment happens in marriage when the husband and/or wife isn't allowed to maintain his or her individuality but is expected to mold to the other's expectations.

Enmeshed families often come together to create enmeshed churches. These churches tend to stifle creativity and stick to rigid traditions that aren't Christ-based. These groups are more interested in defending their "standards" or traditions than seeking truth and living sacrificial love. They sacrifice individuals for the tradition.

If you can see elements of enmeshment in your family, start drawing healthy boundaries. Put your mate and immediate family first. If need be, explain what's happening gently. Get caller ID and don't answer all the calls from excessive callers. Plan a trip away this holiday season. It doesn't have to be far. Nobody in your extended family will die if you aren't there, and your own family will be healthier for it.

> When two individuals are differentiated and secure in their own identities, they can give themselves to one another and become one flesh as God intended. This means that they have a close and stable relationship with their parents and a loyalty to the system in which they were raised, but now they combine their family backgrounds into a new and distinct system.[5]

As for your immediate family, review chapter 9, "Free to Be." Enmeshment is the opposite of individuality. Take the chains of conformity and control off you, your mate, and your kids. Allow yourselves to be who you are and to manifest the strengths God has gifted you with. Allow your children to share their feelings, even if it involves something negative. Support healthy communication and teach grace.

> *Lord, show me if I'm enmeshed with my family of origin or in my immediate family. Give me the insight, wisdom, and strength to draw the lines I need so I can break from enmeshed traditions. Give me the courage to stand strong when boundaries are ignored or criticized. Give me the grace to be who I am in You and offer others the freedom to be the individuals You crafted in Your image.*

Sexual Success

Do not arouse or awaken love until it so desires.

SONG OF SONGS 2:7

Passage: Song of Songs 2

A mother was driving a little girl to her friend's house for a playdate.

"Mommy," the little girl asked, "how old are you?"

"Honey, you're not supposed to ask a lady her age," the mother replied. "It's not polite."

"Okay," the little girl said. "How much do you weigh?"

"Now really," the mother said, "those are personal questions and are really none of your business."

Undaunted, the little girl asked, "Why did you and Daddy get a divorce?"

"That is enough, young lady. Honestly!" The exasperated mother left her daughter at her friend's house and drove away.

The two friends began to play.

"My Mom won't tell me anything about her," the little girl said to her friend.

"Well," said the friend, "all you need to do is look at her driver's license. It's like a report card; it has everything on it."

Later that night the little girl said to her mother, "I know how old you are. You are 32."

The mother was surprised and asked, "How did you find that out?"

The girl answered, "I also know you weigh 140 pounds."

"How did you find that out?" the mother asked again.

"And," the little girl said triumphantly, "I know why you and Daddy got a divorce."

"Oh really?" the mother asked. "Why?"

"Because you got an F in sex."[6]

Most people don't want an "F" in sex. Unfortunately that's how many rate. Making a "good grade" in sex is often dependent on our past sexual experiences. Song of Songs repeatedly mentions not prematurely awakening love. This awakening can come through childhood exposure to hard- or soft-core porn, rape, molestation, or fondling. This early and inappropriate introduction to sexuality plays havoc with the healthy sex life in marriage. Often overwhelming guilt or shame accompanies bad sexual experiences. That guilt cloaks every expression of sexuality. Sex is viewed as something dirty or harmful or scary rather than something beautiful to celebrate with the mate.

Sexual addictions can also come as a result of premature sexual awakening. Many young boys are addicted to porn as young as 8 or 9. Sometimes girls become promiscuous because they were raped or molested. They are starving for someone to love them for who they are, so they turn to the only thing that drew attention to them: sex. Unfortunately, what starts as a cry for love and approval can land some girls (and boys) in prostitution.

Sexual success happens when any negative issues surrounding sexuality are faced head on and dealt with. I understand the shame, guilt, and low self-esteem that torment the soul when someone is molested. But God wants us to be healthy and whole. He can and will heal emotional wounds, including sexual ones. Let God take away the shame, guilt, and paralysis.

In a healthy relationship between husband and wife sex is a vital part of their relationship. The sexual relationship is embraced and celebrated. If one spouse has a lower sex drive than the other, the spouse with the lower drive makes adjustments to fully participate in this important aspect of marriage (often through specialized vitamins, doctor-recommended therapy, counseling, and God's intervention).

What grade are you making in sex these days?

Father, I want my marriage relationship to sizzle. I want to make an "A" in sex. Help me feel comfortable talking to You about sexual issues. I need to thoroughly understand that You created me as a sexual being, and that You want me to function sexually in healthy ways. Please purge my soul and mind of any sexual shame. Teach me to be sexy with my mate and celebrate this gift from You.

Microwave Marriage

When you are on your beds, search your hearts and be silent.

Passage: Psalm 4

Ed was in trouble. He forgot his wedding anniversary and his wife was really mad.

"Tomorrow morning I expect to find a gift in the driveway that goes from 0 to 200 in 6 seconds. *It better be there!*" she told him.

The next morning Ed got up early and left for work. When his wife woke up, she looked out the window. There was a small box gift-wrapped in the middle of the driveway.

Confused, the wife put on her robe, ran out to the driveway, and brought the box back into the house. When she opened it, she found a brand-new bathroom scale.

Funeral services for Ed have been scheduled for Friday.[7]

All marriages have their negative moments. The ideal marriage occurs when both spouses are spiritually mature and have worked through any emotional issues. They've taken care of all negative attitudes and any dysfunctions.

But that's not the way reality works, is it? In the real world people get married when they are far from emotionally and spiritually mature. They have to deal with negative issues as they come up...or avoid them and cause greater rifts. According to David Seamands,

> All those wonderful promises that people make on their wedding day—"I promise to love, care for you, cherish you, through all the circumstances and vicissitudes of life"—these are possible only when a heart is secure

in God's love, grace, and care. Only a forgiven and graced soul can keep such promises. What the person often really means when he says those beautiful words is, "I have a lot of terrific inner needs and inner emptiness and debts to pay, and I'm going to give you a marvelous opportunity to fill my Grand Canyon and take care of me. Aren't I wonderful?"[8]

Robert Hicks puts it like this:

> Most married couples begin with this assumption: "I will marry this person because he/she will make me happy." But what happens when the person is no longer the source or the object of one's happiness? I believe we have looked in the wrong place for happiness and asked our mates, even our children, to give us what only God can give."[9]

No human is capable of never letting someone down. Many times the disappointment isn't caused on purpose but is the result of weaknesses the person has. We have to be ready and quick to give grace and move on. And God will help us do that.

God never fails us. Only He is perfect. Only He is the source of unconditional love and unity. When both spouses stop looking to each other for fulfillment of the soul and start finding that fulfillment in Christ, maturity and stability will come to the marriage. True, a healthy marriage is fulfilling and God made us to desire that fulfillment, but even the best spouses in the world cannot meet the needs of our souls.

We live in a microwave generation; we think we should have everything immediately. But spiritual and emotional growth don't work that way. Neither does marriage. Brian Nystrom says,

> Western culture tends to be result-oriented, and because of this we come to expect our needs and desires to be met quickly. We can become impatient with ourselves or with others if change does not occur rapidly enough for us. For example, we Christians put a lot of emphasis on salvation (which we should), yet at times we put little emphasis on our spiritual journey with God after the conversion experience. Just as our walk with God never ends, so entropy [a measure of disorder] is an issue that will not go away.[10]

The longer we walk with God and the more we allow Him to work on us spiritually and heal us emotionally, the sweeter we grow and the more functional we become. Marriage can either be a continual downward spiral or an upward growth of two hearts beating in tune with the Holy Creator and in tune with each other. Upward growth happens when we continually keep our focus on God.

Lord, the more I learn and the more I seek You, the more I know I need to grow. Please help me let You shine Your piercing light upon my heart and emotions. Show me how I need to change so growth becomes a reality. Right now, Lord, I release any bitterness, resentment, and wrong attitudes that hold me back. Purify my heart daily with Your fire. Purify my marriage. Purify my love for You and my mate.

Healing Infirmities

He took up our infirmities and carried our diseases.

MATTHEW 8:17

Passage: Matthew 8:14-17

Anger Management

Husband: "When I get mad at you, you never fight back. How do you control your anger?"

Wife: "I clean the toilet bowl."

Husband: "How does that help?"

Wife: "I use your toothbrush."[11]

Many people have anger issues that are much like "Old Faithful" at Yellowstone National Park. They spew a never-ending stream of hot emotions upward at regular intervals. The anger is usually the result of issues that have not been dealt with. One pastor testifies that he struggled with anger in his home and marriage for years. He seemed to have little control over the unpredictable outbursts. Finally he realized he'd stuffed his anger from when his father abandoned the family in his childhood.

Anger arises out of childhood abuse, abandonment, and neglect. In such cases, this anger can be considered an infirmity. According to David Seamands,

> In the New Testament, the word *infirmity* was connected with the sacrifices offered by the priests. An infirmity was primarily a physical spot, a

blemish. It was a defect or a deformity either in a man or in an animal...
In the New Testament we begin to see a figurative use of the word
infirmity. It is a metaphor, a figure of speech. The common New Testament word for *infirmity* is the negative form of *sthenos* which means
"strength."...The word is hardly ever used in a purely physical sense in
the New Testament. Rather, it refers to mental, moral, and emotional
weaknesses, to lack of strength. Infirmities in themselves are not sins,
but they do undermine our resistance to temptation. In the New Testament, infirmities are qualities in human nature which may predispose or
incline us to sin, sometimes without any conscious choice on our part.[12]

In our humanity, we all have infirmities. If you have a repeated negative
behavior that you can't seem to get control over, such as outbursts of rage,
it very likely involves infirmities. We can take one of two attitudes toward
our infirmities: 1) "Oh well, God's grace covers this. I'm not going to
worry about it." 2) "I want God to deliver me from my infirmities one by
one, yet I know His grace covers me until they are all dealt with."

While the first statement is absolutely true, an "Oh well" attitude is dangerous. The infirmities that plague us can be the exact things that stunt
growth in our marriages and every other area of our lives—professionally,
spiritually, emotionally, and mentally. Unresolved infirmities can cause
us to be passed over for a promotion or put our spouse in a constant state
of defensiveness.

I've repeatedly watched people who have blatant infirmities wonder why
"all these bad things" happen to them and why they never seem to have
"good luck." They don't see that their own infirmities are creating the problems. Sometimes God can't expand ministries because those in charge of
them are eaten up with infirmities they refuse to allow Him to deal with.
When a person chooses to leave a marriage the other mate is understand-
ably devastated. Nevertheless, many a deserted spouse cannot see that his
or her own infirmities were the cause...nor was the spouse willing to listen
to his or her mate when the problems were brought up. It's like the offend-
ing spouse believes that if he or she didn't *intentionally* do the things that
drove the other spouse away, he or she somehow shouldn't be responsible.

Sometimes these infirmities involve what psychologists call "character disorders." According to Dr. David Hawkins' book *Dealing with the CrazyMakers in Your Life,* these character disorders produce people who are:

* aggressors, who impose their will on you
* egotists, who are too full of themselves to make room for your concerns
* borderlines, who may fly off the handle at any moment
* sufferers, who can't see past their all-consuming woes
* control freaks, who believe their way is the only way[13]

All these people have issues with control, which becomes their underlying infirmity. Whatever the cause, infirmities often create havoc in the lives of others, while the person bearing the infirmities is in hard denial and might very well stay that way unless something horrific happens to open his or her eyes. At times I believe God allows negative dynamics to unfold to show us we have certain infirmities that need to be dealt with. Sometimes these infirmities are huge enough to make others call us CrazyMakers, and sometimes they are the tiny issues that the Lord wants to rid us of in His continual refinement process.

What are your infirmities? Has anybody been trying to communicate with you about a problem area? Has the Lord brought anything up to you? Instead of instantly rejecting or minimizing the criticism, examine your mind, heart, and emotions to see if anything in the criticism might be true. Ask the Lord to show you if the criticism is His way of revealing an infirmity to you. Take time to listen for His wisdom. Jesus Christ is the source of all truth. He will not gloss over truth about yourself to you. Even if it hurts initially, He will reveal your infirmities to you one by one— sometimes during prayer and sometimes through the comments of others. From there, seek God's deliverance.

Lord, please show me any infirmities You want me to work on with You. Remove the blinders of denial, pride, and defensiveness and help me see myself the way You see me. Give me the wisdom to listen to my mate and those around me if they mention an infirmity that needs Your attention...and mine. Unravel the tapestry within me that has created any problems. Make me whole.

Embracing Freedom

In him was life, and that life was the light of men. The light
shines in the darkness, but the darkness has not understood it.

JOHN 1:4-5

Passage: John 1:1-18

During my twenties I worked in a Merle Norman cosmetics studio. I performed a number of responsibilities, including teaching women how to apply makeup. One teaching session will stay in my memory forever. A husband and wife came in together. The whole time I was trying to help the wife with her makeup, the husband required her to turn her face to him at intervals for his inspection and approval. He was highly concerned that she have only the lightest application of makeup. At the same time, he was ogling and making appreciative comments about the picture of a pretty model nearby.

I said, "Yes, she does look stunning, but she's got on way more makeup than you want your wife to wear." I wanted to say more, but didn't. What was going on in this marriage was clearly a case of control.

Both husbands and wives can be guilty of controlling behavior. Sometimes controlling people use Scripture as a tool to validate their authority. Scripture is used as a weapon rather than an instrument of spiritual enlightenment. Christian wives may approach Scripture looking for ways their husbands aren't measuring up. When they find those ways, they take inventory and criticize or demean their husbands. This usually involves husbands not taking equal responsibility for the condition of the home and marriage. Also, in putting down their spouses, wives are elevating themselves to judge. Husbands also approach the Bible looking for ways to take control. They use key verses to create concepts and roles that limit their wives in many ways...and certainly in ways they would never want applied to them.

The Bible was never intended as a weapon to wound others or put marriages in chains. It was intended as a pathway to spiritual empowerment and, in marriage, as a handbook for getting a little bit of heaven on earth. As you read the words of Christ, pray that He will free your life and your marriage of any darkness and open you and your spouse's minds to His way of thinking. Only in this mind-set can you fully embrace the freedom found in Christ and reach the potential heaven in your marriage.

Lord, please daily deliver me from any thought processes that cause me to read Your Word in a way contrary to Your heart. Forgive me for the times I've used the Bible to my own advantage. Help me take a fresh look at the Word and its liberating power. Free me from any need to control as I relinquish control to You and seek to put others before me.

Fixing Financial Friction

Keep your lives from the love of money and be con-
tent with what you have, because God has said,
"Never will I leave you; never will I forsake you."
So we say with confidence, "The Lord is my helper; I
will not be afraid. What can man do to me?"

HEBREWS 13:5-6

Passage: Hebrews 13

I recently held a marriage conference where I got to spend time with the coordinator and her husband. They were an emotionally and spiritually savvy young team who had a lot going for them. One thing they had decided was that if they ever came to a place where they needed counseling, they'd go for it. That time came with money issues. The wife was resentful because her husband wouldn't help pay the bills. But during counseling she realized she'd taken on too much of the financial responsibility because of her control and trust issues.

For many couples, money is a battleground. One spouse may want to live week to week and not worry about long-term savings, and the other may want a fully mapped financial plan for decades into the future. If one partner is a spendthrift, the other might be a miser. Often these tendencies are rooted in childhood experiences. For instance, one man details how his wife was raised to believe that when you get your paycheck, you spend it with no consideration of the month's bills. When it came time to pay the bills, there wasn't any money because the wife had spent funds on pleasure items. The man, who was a miser, blew up.

Sometimes couples use finances as an issue of territory. It's really not about money or even managing money. It's about power and control. Holding the purse strings means the other spouse has to ask for money or be accountable for every penny spent.

In some marriages there are extenuating circumstances that transcend "normal" money issues. For instance, some psychological disorders, such as being bi-polar, can perpetuate spending compulsions. In these cases, medication and professional therapy are viable options. If an addiction to gambling, alcohol, drugs, pornography, or shopping is sucking the bank account dry, not confronting the problem and not demanding the addict get help perpetuates the addiction and exacerbates the financial impact. Addiction needs to be dealt with through therapy, honesty, and boundaries.

Many times financial issues can be resolved through healthy compromise, communication, and not viewing money as a territory issue. A good place to start is for husbands and wives to sit down together and detail what their individual money management styles currently are and explain their financial education experience growing up. Then they can discuss and come to a mutual agreement of what a healthy balance would be. This mutual agreement might include making sure all the bills are paid before extras can be purchased, agreeing to a certain percentage for general savings, general giving, giving to church, saving for children's expenses, and saving for retirement. Furthermore, couples need to decide if bill paying will be a split responsibility or which person will take charge of this area.

In our marriage, there have been times when my husband paid all the bills (which he hated) or I paid all the bills (which I hated less than he). When we both had home-based businesses, we divided our responsibilities. Daniel had complete financial autonomy for his home-based business. I had complete autonomy for mine. We each pay for a portion of the domestic bills. This worked well for us during that season of our lives. We've also pooled our money, which worked well when needed.

In healthy marriages, couples come to an agreement of what works for them. If one spouse is a whiz with finances, that one should use his or her gift in the marriage while taking into consideration the feelings, opinions, and needs of his or her mate. If neither spouse is good with money or the couple can't work through the problems alone, a financial counselor might be a wise and viable option.

God is more interested in you and your spouse having a personal relationship with Him and a thriving marriage than having every penny accounted for.

> *Dear Lord, teach me to put my relationship with my mate at top priority in my life after You. Teach me to relinquish control of my finances to You since You are the source of everything. Show me how my mate and I can manage our money in ways that glorify You.*

And Then There Were Children

Sons are a heritage from the LORD,
children a reward from him.

PSALM 127:3

Passage: Psalm 127

Children forever change a home and a couple's relationship!

Jesus Christ said, "Let the little children come to me, and do not hinder them, for the kingdom of heaven belongs to such as these" (Matthew 19:14). He also said, "Unless you change and become like little children, you will never enter the kingdom of heaven. Therefore, whoever humbles himself like this child is the greatest in the kingdom of heaven. And whoever welcomes a little child like this in my name welcomes me" (Matthew 18:3-5). With this understanding, we as adults need to value our children and forever strive to be childlike in our trust in Christ but not childish in our behavior, especially in relation to our own kids. If parents aren't careful the child issue can splinter or destroy their marriage. This is a tragedy! There can be a healthy balance between cherishing children without allowing them to override the marital relationship.

When Christ is truly the center of the home, each member has value. Children are given room to be who they are and to develop the capability to think for themselves. It's safe for them to reveal their thoughts and emotions. Children who grow up with parents who value them as human beings created in the image of God arrive into adulthood with healthy self-esteem and a strong belief in themselves and who they are in Christ.

They also are equipped to have healthy marriages and become balanced parents themselves.

However, children who are habitually protected from the consequences of their own choices may grow up to be dependents who never quite leave home. Sometimes they become "takers," adults who are in the habit of taking everything anyone will give them while never giving themselves. They make decisions that hurt others and never realize they should apologize or make restitution because they can't see past themselves. Other times, kids may morph into full-blown criminals, perhaps because they never had firm boundaries at home.

Many parents fall into the pattern of trying to protect a child from the other parent. Sometimes this comes because one parent is a stricter disciplinarian than the other. So the other spouse "covers" for the child by taking responsibility for what the child has done or by defending or protecting the child. In these cases parenting is not balanced. One is too strict, and the other enables negative behavior in the child to protect from the "authority" parent. This throws the parents into a never-ending cycle. The strict parent gets tougher to try to compensate for the enabling parent, which throws the enabling parent into even more protecting behaviors. These patterns exist in nonblended families and blended families. In blended families, the biological parent often feels toxic guilt in relation to a divorce or other family issues. He or she might allow the children to "get away with murder" due to guilt.

Neither parent should have an "I rule" attitude. Neither should parents allow the children to rule. (And kids will naturally try. It's human nature!) Parents need to come together and work out a parenting plan they both agree upon. They need to determine in advance that they will back up each other's authority and not override the other parent's decisions without discussing the decision with him or her. When one parent claims all or most of the authority over the children, the other parent tends to compensate with permissiveness or sympathy, which perpetuates generational dysfunction. Sometimes he or she does this without realizing the dynamics of what's happening. One man told me he felt like a "cage cleaner" at a zoo and nothing else. His wife, a homeschool mom, ran a tight ship at home and didn't give him a lot of input on the parenting. Likewise, wives can be cut out of the parenting equation by husbands who insist they are "large and in charge." According to Brian Nystrom,

> Parenting direction and decision making must be done on a mutual, agreed-upon basis for all matters. There can be no abuse or neglect of the children. Unilateral parenting decisions cause marital desanctification, because they remove one spouse from the mutual decision making necessary for a healthy marriage. Rough treatment will also cause marital desanctification. Marital sanctification occurs when all aspects of parenting are done mutually or by mutual agreement and the children are treated lovingly and respectfully.[14]

This type of parenting takes two people who are willing to talk through the issues and compromise. It initially requires more effort but eventually leads to great harmony in the home and marriage. The children live with healthy boundaries that have reasonable consequences and are supported by both parents. The kids are then more likely to grow into functional adults.

Dear Lord, please teach me to value unity as a spouse and as a parent. Show me anything I am doing that perpetuates a dysfunctional pattern in my parenting. Help me and my spouse merge our minds and hearts on the issues of parenting. Teach me how to compromise and stick with our predetermined guidelines.

Building on the Rock

*Therefore everyone who hears these words of mine and puts them
into practice is like a wise man who built his house on the rock.*

MATTHEW 7:24

Passage: Matthew 7:24-29

We once lived in a home with a retainer wall that was poorly constructed.
This wall was approximately five feet tall and ran along the south side of
the pool. While the bulging creosote timbers told us it would eventually
collapse, we didn't expect it to do so within a year of our moving in. However, a wet spring was all it took. I went out one morning to see the wall
had fallen apart. Big, square timbers and red earth were scattered everywhere. We immediately called an expert to build a sturdier wall.

Marriages are a lot like that retainer wall. If they are built upon unhealthy
concepts, unbalanced principles, or an era in culture, they'll collapse when
the storms come. Jesus told a parable about a house built on sand and one
built on rock. When the rains came the house built on the sand collapsed.
The house built on the rock remained firm.

Jesus Christ is that rock. Marriages built on His teachings have a foundation that is not going to shudder when strong winds blow in. And storms
come against all marriages at one time or another.

If your marriage is on the verge of collapsing, examine the foundation. Just
as we're rebuilding our retainer wall, so your marriage can be rebuilt and
strengthened by establishing a new foundation in full alignment with the
teachings of Christ. During your reconstruction, remember...

In everything, do to others what you would have them do to you (Matthew 7:12).

Ask and it will be given to you, seek and you will find; knock and the door will be opened to you. For everyone who asks receives; he who seeks finds; and to him who knocks, the door will be opened (Matthew 7:7-8).

And he said: "I tell you the truth, unless you change and become like little children, you will never enter the kingdom of heaven. Therefore, whoever humbles himself like this child is the greatest in the kingdom of heaven" (Matthew 18:3-4).

This is My commandment, that you love one another, just as I have loved you (John 15:12 NASB).

So [Jesus] got up from the meal, took off his outer clothing, and wrapped a towel around his waist. After that, he poured water into a basin and began to wash his disciples' feet, drying them with the towel that was wrapped around him (John 13:4-5).

Lord, align my marriage with Your heart and mind. Help me to actively live out Your words. Convict me, Father, when I fall short. Forever illuminate my path with Your light and Your wisdom.

Are You Ready for a Revolution?

1. *Merriam-Webster's 11ᵗʰ Collegiate Dictionary,* electronic version (Springfield, MA: Merriam-Webster, Inc., 2003), s.v. "Revolution."

Chapter 1—Encountering the Revolutionary

1. Gary and Barbara Rosberg, *The Five Love Needs of Men and Women* (Wheaton, IL: Tyndale, 2000), 8.
2. David Hawkins, Ph.D., *The Relationship Doctor's Prescription for Better Communication in Your Marriage* (Eugene, OR: Harvest House, 2007), 27.
3. Virginia Satir, *Peoplemaking* (Palo Alto, CA: Science and Behavior Books, 1972), n.p.

Chapter 2—Living Sacrifices

1. Joseph Coleson, "Gender Equality: The Biblical Imperative," Neil B. Wiseman, ed., *Preacher's Magazine* (Kansas City: Nazarene Publishing House, 2000), March/April/May 2000, vol. 75, no. 3, 8.
2. Judson W. Van DeVenter, "I Surrender All," *Worship in Song* (Kansas City, MO: Lillenas Publishing Company, 1972), 287, public domain.
3. Robert M. Hicks, *The Christian Family in Changing Times: The Myths, Models, and Mystery of Family Life* (Grand Rapids, MI: Baker Books, 2002), 57.
4. David and Vera Mace, *Marriage: East and West* (Garden City, NY: Doubleday Dolphin Books, 1960), 30-31.
5. Jack O. Balswick and Judith K. Balswick, *The Family: A Christian Perspective on the Contemporary Home,* 2ⁿᵈ ed. (Grand Rapid, MI: Baker Books, 1999), 79.
6. Brian Nystrom, MSW, *Ordinary People, ExtraOrdinary Marriages: Reclaiming God's Design for Oneness* (San Jose, CA: Writer's Showcase, 2001), 60.
7. David A. Seamands, *Healing for Damaged Emotions* in comp. *Healing Your Heart of Painful Emotions* (Edison, NJ: Inspirational Press, 1993), 18.

Chapter 3—When Jesus Meets Our Issues

1. Author unknown, "Words Women Use," received via e-mail, n.d.
2. David A. Seamands, *Healing for Damaged Emotions* in comp. *Healing Your Heart of Painful Emotions* (Edison, NJ: Inspirational Press, 1993), 12-13.
3. Ibid., 11.
4. Ibid., 10-11.

5. William Blake, "The Lamb," *The English Romantics: Major Poetry and Critical Theory,* John L. Mahoney, ed. (Lexington, PA: D.C. Heath and Company, 1978), 29-30.

6. David Hawkins, Ph.D., *When Pleasing People Is Hurting You: Finding God's Patterns for Healthy Relationships* (Eugene, OR: Harvest House Publishers, 2004), 35.

7. Robert Subby, *Beyond Codependency* (San Francisco: Harper & Row Publishers, 1989), 16.

Chapter 4—Ruling and Drooling

1. Brian Nystrom, MSW, *Ordinary People, ExtraOrdinary Marriages: Reclaiming God's Design for Oneness* (San Jose, CA: Writer's Showcase, 2001), 67.

2. James Strong, "Oy-kod-es-pot-eh'-o," 3616, "Greek Dictionary of the New Testament," *The New Strong's Exhaustive Concordance of the Bible* by James Strong, LL.D., S.T.D. (Nashville, TN: Thomas Nelson Publishers, 1990), 51. Note: See also number 3617: "oy-kod-es-pot'-ace."

3. David A. Seamands, *Healing for Damaged Emotions,* in comp. *Healing Your Heart of Painful Emotions* (Edison, NJ: Inspirational Press, 1993), 43.

4. Ibid.

5. Judy Cornelia Pearson and Paul Edward Nelson, *Understanding and Sharing: An Introduction to Speech Communication* (Dubuque, IA: Wm. C. Brown Publishers, 1988), 51.

6. Elizabeth O'Connor, *Eighth Day of Creation* (Waco, TX: Word Books, 1971), 59.

Chapter 5—Leading and Following

1. Merriam-Webster's 11th Collegiate Dictionary, electronic version (Springfield, MA: Merriam-Webster, Inc., 2003), s.v. "leader."

2. Ibid., s.v. "leadership."

3. Joseph Coleson, "Gender Equality: The Biblical Imperative," Neil B. Wiseman, ed., *Preacher's Magazine* (Kansas City, MO: Nazarene Publishing House, 2000), March/April/May 2000, vol. 75, no. 3, 7.

4. Kenneth Barker, gen. ed., *Reflecting God Study Bible* (Grand Rapids, MI: Zondervan, 1995), s.v. Romans 16:1.

5. Bob and Yvonne Turnball, *TeamMates, Building Your Marriage to Complete, Not Compete* (Kansas City, MO: Beacon Hill Press of Kansas City), 60-61.

6. David A. Seamands, *Healing for Damaged Emotions,* in comp. *Healing Your Heart of Painful Emotions* (Edison, NJ: Inspirational Press, 1993), 29.

Chapter 6—Healthy Balance

1. Robert M. Hicks, *The Christian Family in Changing Times: The Myths, Models, and Mystery of Family Life* (Grand Rapids, MI: Baker Books, 2002), 62.

2. *The New Lexicon Webster's Dictionary of the English Language* (New York: Lexicon Publications, 1989), s.v. "lead."

3. Hicks, *Christian Family in Changing Times,* 60.
4. Kenneth Barker, gen. ed., *Reflecting God Study Bible* (Grand Rapids, MI: Zondervan, 1995), s.v. Genesis 2:18.
5. Joseph E. Coleson, *'Ezer Cenegdo: A Power like Him, Facing Him as Equal* (Grantham, PA: Wesleyan-Holiness Women Clergy, 1996).
6. Lawrence O. Richards, *The Victor Bible Background Commentary: New Testament* (Colorado Springs: Victor Books, 1994), 395.
7. Ibid.
8. Brian Nystrom, MSW, *Ordinary People, ExtraOrdinary Marriages: Reclaiming God's Design for Oneness* (San Jose, CA: Writer's Showcase, 2001), 56, 61.

Chapter 7—Marriage Paradox

1. Jack O. Balswick and Judith K. Balswick, *The Family: A Christian Perspective on the Contemporary Home,* 2nd ed. (Grand Rapid, MI: Baker Books, 1999), 79.
2. Donald M. Joy and Robbie B. Joy, *Two Become One: God's Blueprint for Couples* (Napanee, IN: Evangel Publishing House, 2002), 129-30.
3. Ibid., 87.
4. Joseph Coleson, "Gender Equality: The Biblical Imperative," Neil B. Wiseman, ed., *Preacher's Magazine* (Kansas City: Nazarene Publishing House, 2000), March/April/May 2000, vol. 75, no. 3, 7.
5. Joy and Joy, *Two Become One,* 129.
6. Steve Mensing, M.Ed., "Passive-Aggressive Personality Cluster," emoclear.com/clusters/passiveaggressive.html.
7. Adapted from ibid.

Chapter 8—The Sex Question

1. Author unknown, "Dear Diary," received via e-mail.
2. David A. Seamands, *Healing for Damaged Emotions,* in comp. *Healing Your Heart of Painful Emotions* (Edison, NJ: Inspirational Press, 1993), 18.
3. Bill and Pam Farrel, *Red-Hot Monogamy: Making Your Marriage Sizzle* (Eugene, OR: Harvest House Publishers, 2006), 16.
4. Seamands, *Healing for Damaged Emotions,* 17.
5. Ralph H. Earle Jr. and Mark R. Laaser, *The Pornography Trap: Setting Pastors and Laypersons Free from Sexual Addictions* (Kansas City: Beacon Hill Press of Kansas City, 2002), 13.
6. Ibid., 13.
7. Mike Courtney, New Life Coaching, www.new-lifecoaching.com.
8. Earle Jr. and Laaser, *The Pornography Trap,* 25.
9. Ibid., 45.

10. Dr. David E. Clarke, *Cinderella Meets the Caveman: Stop the Boredom in Your Marriage and Jump-Start the Passion* (Eugene, OR: Harvest House Publishers, 2007), 162-63.

11. Marla Taviano, *Is That All He Thinks About? How to Enjoy Great Sex with Your Husband* (Eugene, OR: Harvest House Publishers, 2007), 72.

12. Earle Jr. and Laaser, *The Pornography Trap*, 13.

Chapter 9—Free to Be

1. Brian Nystrom, MSW, *Ordinary People, ExtraOrdinary Marriages: Reclaiming God's Design for Oneness* (San Jose, CA: Writer's Showcase, 2001), 15-16.

2. Robert M. Hicks, *The Christian Family in Changing Times: The Myths, Models, and Mystery of Family Life* (Grand Rapids, MI: Baker Books, 2002), 57.

3. Author unknown, "How to Make a Woman Happy," received via e-mail.

4. Dr. David E. Clarke, *Cinderella Meets the Caveman: Stop the Boredom in Your Marriage and Jump-Start the Passion* (Eugene, OR: Harvest House Publishers, 2007), 158.

5. Ibid., 157.

6. Gary Smalley with John Trent, *Love Is a Decision* (Dallas: Word Publishing, 1989), 51.

7. Scott Farhart, M.D., *Intimate & Unashamed: What Every Man and Woman Need to Know* (Lake Mary, FL: Siloam, 2003), 14.

8. Bill and Pam Farrel, *Red-Hot Monogamy: Making Your Marriage Sizzle* (Eugene, OR: Harvest House Publishers, 2006), 160.

9. Hicks, *Christian Family in Changing Times*, 56.

Revolution Reflections

1. Author unknown, "Poison Mushrooms," received via e-mail.

2. David A. Seamands, *Healing for Damaged Emotions*, in comp. *Healing Your Heart of Painful Emotions* (Edison, NJ: Inspirational Press, 1993), 19.

3. Author unknown, "The Husband Store," received via e-mail.

4. David Hawkins, Ph.D., *When Pleasing People Is Hurting You: Finding God's Patterns for Healthy Relationships* (Eugene, OR: Harvest House Publishers, 2004), 116-17.

5. Jack O. Balswick and Judith K. Balswick, *The Family: A Christian Perspective on the Contemporary Home*, 2nd ed. (Grand Rapid, MI: Baker Books, 1999), 77.

6. Author unknown, "F in Sex," received via e-mail.

7. Author unknown, "Bathroom Scale," received via e-mail.

8. Seamands, *Healing for Damaged Emotions*, 29.

9. Robert Hicks, *The Christian Family in Changing Times: The Myths, Models, and Mystery of Family Life* (Grand Rapids, MI: Baker Books, 2002), 66.

10. Brian Nystrom, MSW, *Ordinary People, ExtraOrdinary Marriages: Reclaiming God's Design for Oneness* (San Jose, CA: Writer's Showcase, 2001), 51.

11. Author unknown, "Anger Management," received via e-mail.

12. Seamands, *Healing for Damaged Emotions,* 34.

13. David Hawkins, Ph.D., *Dealing with the CrazyMakers in Your Life: Setting Boundaries on Unhealthy Relationships* (Eugene, OR: Harvest House Publishers, 2007), back cover.

14. Nystrom, *Ordinary People, ExtraOrdinary Marriages,* 95.

About the Author

Debra White Smith continues to impact and entertain readers with her life-changing books, including *101 Ways to Romance Your Marriage, Romancing Your Husband,* and *Romancing Your Wife.* She's also an award-winning novelist and has written many books including The Sisters Suspense series, The Austen series, and The Debutantes series. She's won such honors as Top-10 Reader Favorite, Gold Medallion finalist, and Retailer's Choice Award finalist. Debra has more than 50 books to her credit and over a million books in print.

The founder of Real Life Ministries, Debra speaks passionately with insight and humor at ministry events across the nation. Debra has been featured on a variety of media, including *The 700 Club, At Home Life, Getting Together, Moody Broadcasting Network, Fox News, Viewpoint,* and *America's Family Coaches.* She holds an M.A. in English.

Debra lives in small-town America with her husband, two children, two dogs, and a herd of cats.

To write Debra or contact her for speaking engagements, check out her website:

www.debrawhitesmith.com

or send mail to

Real Life Ministries
Daniel W. Smith, Ministry Manager
PO Box 1482
Jacksonville, TX 75766

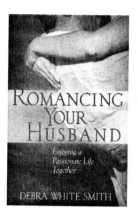

ROMANCING YOUR HUSBAND

Early days in a relationship are exhilarating, but they can't touch the thrilling love affair you can have now. Cutting through traditional misconceptions and exploring every facet of the Bible's message on marriage, *Romancing Your Husband* reveals how you can create a union others only dream about. From making Jesus an active part of your marriage to arranging fantastic romantic interludes, you'll discover how to—

- make romance a reality
- "knock your husband's socks off"
- become a lover-wife, not a mother-wife
- find freedom in forgiving
- cultivate a sacred romance with God

Experience fulfillment through romancing your husband...and don't be surprised when he romances you back!

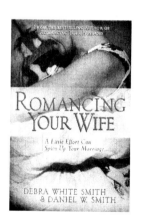

ROMANCING YOUR WIFE

by Debra White Smith and Daniel W. Smith

Do you want your husband to surprise you and put more romance in your relationship? *Romancing Your Wife* can help! Give this book to your hubby, and he'll discover ways to create an exciting, enthusiastic marriage.

Debra and her husband, Daniel, offer biblical wisdom and practical advice that when put into practice will help your husband mentally, emotionally, and physically improve his relationship with you. He'll discover tools to build a dynamite marriage, including how to—

- communicate his love more effectively
- make you feel cherished
- better understand your needs and wants
- create a unity of spirit and mind
- increase the passion in your marriage

From insights on little things that jazz up a marriage to more than 20 "Endearing Encounters," *Romancing Your Wife* sets the stage for love and romance.

More Great Books
by Debra White Smith

FICTION

The Austen Series
Amanda
Central Park
First Impressions
Northpointe Chalet
Possibilities
Reason & Romance

The Debutantes
Heather
Lorna (March 2008)

**The Seven Sisters Series/
Sisters Suspense Series**
Second Chances
The Awakening/Picture Perfect
A Shelter in the Storm
To Rome with Love
For Your Eyes Only
This Time Around
Let's Begin Again

Fiction/Parable
The Richest Person in the World (with Stan Toler)

NONFICTION
101 Ways to Romance Your Marriage
Romancing Your Husband
Romancing Your Wife
What Jane Austen Taught Me About Love and Romance

the tie that binds

a conference about love....

For more information about
The Tie That Binds...A Conference About Love
or if you are interested in hosting a conference in
your church, please contact us at:
www.3strandsministries.com
www.tiethatbinds.org

Lorica is a worship band that was formed in 1999 to serve as worship leaders of College Place Baptist Church in Monroe, La. We are comprised of six common people with common talents that have been forged into something very special through our commitment to the Almighty God and to the worship that brings glory to His name. Our goal has always been and will always be to lead God's people to His throne through the wonderful gift he gave us in worship. The name Lorica is derived from a poem written by St. Patrick in the 15th century that speaks of being completely surrounded with Christ. It is our prayer that everything we do, leads people to a closer and deeper relationship with the Giver of Life, Jesus Christ.

The title song of this project, "The Tie That Binds", is our offering to anyone who is married, ever been married, or ever will be married. Christian marriages have never been under attack more than they are today. This song reaches out with a reality that there are struggles and troubled times. But it also presents the solution to those times being a relationship rooted in Jesus Christ, for He is the tie that binds. It is our prayer that through this study and through this song that God will bless you and your marriage. Worship Him and may you be surrounded with Christ through the heart and message of this song!

To download the song "The Tie That Binds" go to
www.loricamusic.com

A cord of three strands is not easily broken...Ecclesiastes 4:12